Semi-Detached

A Play

David Turner

Samuel French—London
New York—Sydney—Toronto—Hollywood

AUTHOR'S NOTE TO PRODUCERS

This play is a satire in the Classical tradition—but don't let that put anybody off! It is a design for laughter and should be played as a huge piece of fun, a romp. Above all, it is deliberately theatrical, a showy piece of bravura. It invites exaggeration, pace and panache. The producer is recommended to think in terms of the popular theatre from Aristophanes to the music hall comedian's script.

Despite the long ancestry of the Classical Comedy, the modern stage is rather unfamiliar with many of its conventions, owing to the unfortunate pre-eminence of the naturalistic play in this century. Let me enlarge, therefore, upon the implications of the Classical form.

The Action

A main device of Classical Comedy is the *imbroglio*; the plot is knotted and reknotted so that the audience wonders how it will ever be untied or shaken loose again. Consequently, the presentation should be clearly aware of this guessing game which holds the audience's attention. At times the dialogue makes a revision of the complexities of the plot but this is not, in itself, sufficient to maintain a full audience response. The actors should play their roles on behalf of the audience and be aware that they are not on the stage merely to be observed but to divert, entertain and lead the audience in an understanding of the complications and unravelling of the plot. They should play outwards to the spectators, embracing the merriment, standing midway between their laughter and the text, enjoying themselves in demonstrating the flow of the action with its ridiculous situations.

It is not solely the demands of the action which cause me to recommend a manner of acting which is associated with farce; there is another reason which I shall mention later. But since farce immediately suggests itself and the term seems to have an inhibiting effect upon certain directors today, I feel some clarification is necessary.

Some critics of the drama, whose sole critical activity consists of the shuffling and affixing of a few well-worn labels, use farce as a term of deprecation and a fashionable, almost snobbish, attitude towards the convention is often assumed. But what determines the importance of a farce is the cause of the reduction of a human being to absurdity; it can be a loss of trousers, it can be the accepted philosophy of contemporary society. If the producer requires literary authority for the form, let him recall that Molière and Jonson raised farce to the level of great art.

Even so, I hope that farcical is an inadequate description of the play in which I have attempted to use the whole range of comic devices from the comedy of situation to linguistic conceits. The play aims to be continuously comic, gaining variety by involving the audience in a series of comic effects, so that every mood and temperament is engaged in the comic vision. As the play proceeds, each member of the audience passes on his laughter to his neighbour. The members of the audience educate each other in comedy. It is a cumulative process.

Yet I can foresee that a director, timid of letting the play speak for itself and feeling that he must justify his own social attitudes to the audience, may be tempted to impose upon the work a tone of serious moral condemnation. He may claim that too much laughter indicates that the shafts of satire have not gone home. He may decide to limit the laughter by cutting laugh lines or by running through them without pause to allow the audience to respond. Such a humourless approach to the play would be foolish and disastrous. I do not see how people can laugh without first seeing the point, and we must all be aware that without humour, satire too readily becomes self-satisfying invective. The audience would develop a feeling of frustration if it wished to laugh but was prevented continually from doing so. More importantly, without laughter, the members of the audience would feel they had been observing the machinations of a corrupt family which is outside them. Without free laughter, their only response would be to share in the sneering superiority of the director himself and this they might be unwilling to do.

This is popular comedy. The audience should not feel it is outside the play; the presentation cannot function properly without the audience's involvement and participation through a ready supply of mirth. Laughter is an admission of human failure, as witnessed on the stage; our laughter is evidence of our recognition that the immorality and hypocrisy of the Midways is in some part our own. The response to this play must be immediate and direct and the response aimed at is laughter.

The Characters

It is important to recognize that the characters are neither real people nor naturalistic portraits. They are caricatures or personifications of contemporary types. As in the older comedies, their names suggest their identities.

"Midway" indicates someone who is on a journey, half-way between places. In this case, the Midway family has left the realm of the socially underprivileged and is travelling towards their ideal dream world of graceful living. The Hadfield family denotes those who are on their way down; they once had the *field* or sphere of social importance, but are now about to be superseded by the ambitious Midways. Makepiece, the wealthy factory-owner, stands outside this social battle, for he makes that which is of prime importance, "pieces" or money. In another sense, he is a purely theatrical figure, being the *deus ex machina* and thus making the piece or completing the play. Freeman indicates a person who is at liberty to choose; his choice is either love or money.

It must be accepted by the cast at the outset that the play requires the representation of personality traits or humours rather than "living the parts". They should "put on" or "personate" the characters rather than "be" them. The world of *Semi-Detached* is all too familiar to the majority of the audience and it is the attempt of this play to cause a re-examination of the known and accepted by presenting it in heightened terms. In one way it is the everyday world under a magnifying glass; in another, it is the behaviour of our time laid bare by showing such vices as selfishness, duplicity and greed free from their usual social camouflage. These two demands suggest that the acting should be larger than life and yet contain the utmost of precision and economy. This is my other reason for recommending a style which is allied to farce.

Many actors today have been trained almost exclusively in a naturalistic method of performance. "Feeling the part" is regarded as an essential of acting. Consequently, they have a sense of bereavement and resentment when told that these parts must be played superficially. I should like to encourage them to believe that instead of demonstrating psychological depth and character development, they have, in this kind of play, an opportunity of displaying through personality, technique and virtuosity, their ability to manipulate and dominate the response of the audience. The leading actor, in particular, should perhaps regard his part as a vast variety of imitations or burlesques. He personates Fred at being smug, anxious, frenetic, tender, authoritative, humble, and so on. Each scene should be examined for the essential attitude of Fred and then it should be played in large, clear and economic terms.

One aspect of Fred which runs through the whole of the play is his abounding energy. He is around fifty and yet assumes the dynamic of a man half his age. Further than this, the urgent activity and display of potency of the man must be exaggerated in playing. A very practical point, therefore, is that the role should be given to an actor who as a person indicates a reserve of energy. That the actor is himself younger than the character he is presenting may assist rather than detract from the style of the play. As I have explained, the actors should "personate" the roles rather than "be" them. An actor, younger than Fred, would have to "put on" the appearance of an older yet energetic man. This may add to the feeling of caricature and leave the audience in no doubt that these people are not real, but theatrical inventions.

Fred is a salesman, a product and a victim of our age. Enthusiasm, organization of others, an appearance of sincerity, determination to win, sham-praise and counterfeit sympathy are some of the ingredients of successful selling which he has gained from his correspondence courses and added to his personality "line-up". There are, however, a few moments in the play when the audience should feel there is a human anxiety behind the façade. These occur: in the second act when he admits to his wife his failure in assuming a public-school appearance; towards the end of this act when for a moment he loses control and examines his inner conflicts; and at the end of the third act when he reflects on the nature of "honesty" and asks, "Is it?" to his wife's suggestion that it is a wonderful world. These brief glimpses into the heart of Fred are of the highest importance, for they indicate he is aware of his own knavery and hypocrisy; like most of us he has an inner doubt of the sincerity of the social role he is playing, but he will play on, for he was born to this culture and can live only within its framework. These insights allow us to recognize he is a representation of humanity in an affluent society. I sympathize with Fred, the everyman of our commercial times; I want the audience to sympathize with him, too. Only by feeling he has somewhere a heart can we think of him as a victim and hate the forces that have made him so. It is not Fred I condemn, but our culture.

In a sense, the other characters are an extension of Fred; they represent jointly the society which has created him.

Hilda, his wife, is possessed by a fear of slipping back to those underprivileged areas of society from which she has emerged. Her "refined" speech and new-found tokens of superiority are necessary for her own reassurance. Without Hilda's admiration and encouragement, Fred would never have found the courage to go on seeking advancement. She is essentially a good woman, loyal to her husband, recognizing him as the leader; she has never wanted to break herself of the working-class lore which demands that father should come first. She tries desperately to hold the family together. When, at the end of the play, she accepts Eileen's departure, it is because Eileen herself renounces her membership of the family group. As with all the characters, her particular personality traits, smugness, ambition for her husband and high regard for respectability, must be played in ridiculous proportions. Throughout her amoral intrigues the audience must feel a sympathy for this loving and doting mother. They must ask themselves indulgently, "How else could one behave in that situation?" The fact that they are also laughing at her indicates that they might reserve to themselves another solution.

Tom represents a cruder image of the family selfishness. He is that part of the younger generation in the affluent society which wants little responsibility, is comfortable, rather aimless, and quite content to sit back and let itself be provided for by others. A healthy animal, a pleasant, easy-going lad who needs to be forced into action.

Avril represents boldly the selfishness of the family. If she cannot have her way she will use as blackmail an unseemly display of hysterics.

Eileen must be played as a caricature as much as the rest. She is not really a sincere person; she talks too much about honour, integrity and truth for that. She is her own ideal; she wants to be different; she cannot conform. She is another aspect of the second generation of the affluent working-class; she is a left-wing prig.

Garnet Hadfield, as her Christian name suggests, is semi-precious. She has a so-called cultured voice, peculiar, I find, to those women who rather like to have the rest of the world hear them vociferating in restaurants and other public places. Her son, *Nigel*, has attended a rather minor public school where he acquired the "right" accent but little else. The pair of them represent the weaker and failing elements of the Establishment, which are, of course, fair game to Fred.

Makepiece stands for power, riches, influence and authentic self-confidence . . . everything, in fact, which Fred would like to acquire. "He is so rich, he is beyond it all." He should be much more relaxed than anyone else in the play. All the same, he is a god out of a three-litre, not out of a heavenly car. He has the fear of mortality and it is this that Fred plays upon in the end. The discussion Fred has with Makepiece on how to increase his life expectation should be whispered, anxious and secretive. For here is the comprehensive absurdity, the heart of the satirical intention, the thing that Fred knows but only in moments of extreme emergency will openly hint at: our struggles for status, our desire for power, our frenzied attempts to be important are all ridiculous when we become aware that soon we are going to die. This is the madness and fear Fred feels in the obsessed section at the end of Act Two when he says it is "The day I've always dreaded . . . the brain refuses to fight any more". By an irony, he uses his own fear of death to exploit a similar terror in Makepiece during the closing stages of the play.

Robert Freeman is an incipient Fred. As the action progresses we should find he has certain gestures and mannerisms which are similar to those of the protagonist. This culminates in the third act in parallel movements of the mentor and his disciple.

The Movement

This play requires a modern adaptation of that style of movement which is usually associated with Restoration Comedy. The *core* of the actors' gestures should be magnified to ridiculous proportions and all else shorn away. Similarly, the relationship of characters to each other on the stage and their movement during the scenes should present the exaggerated *essence* of the relationship and the movement. This method makes not only the most familiar movements appear absurd but it is also satirical in purpose, for it attempts to show the stark, unvarnished truth within human behaviour and hold it up to ridicule. The total effect should be that of an ever-changing, bold, geometrical or mathematical dance. It stresses that these people are caricatures or puppets.

This style must be established from the very beginning. The modern audience is not familiar with it. It is for this reason I have made the exposition at the opening of the play rather lengthy. The audience has to be won over to the manner of the playing before the complications of the action can start. The speech about cars is a dramatist's trick. I know that most of our theatre-goers will react to jokes about their vehicles, but while their attention is being arrested by the speech, Fred, through his movements, should be setting the style which is to be accepted throughout the play. He should make the gestures I describe and at the same time address the audience, welcoming them into a relationship in which he will be personifying a role on their behalf.

It will be noticed that there are times in the text when I have suggested that lines should be delivered directly to the audience. The actors, however, should find many others for themselves. It is up to them to decide through their own technique where best to engage the confidence of the spectators.

The Setting

The classical and satirical approach should be seen also in the setting. It is necessary for the designer to ask himself what are the essential factors of a post-war semi-detached house and its decoration. These major factors should then be exaggerated and minor accompaniments from other styles omitted.

To economize on materials and labour, these houses are usually square in form and flimsy in structure. Panelled doors have given way to the flush variety with hardboard surfaces and cardboard packing. To justify and sell this cheapness and frugality, the builders have introduced such terms as "open plan", "Scandinavian look" and emphasize the neat, clean lines of modern living. They have attempted to disguise the cheerless functionalism by using strong colours in the decoration.

The task of the designer, then, is to suggest to the audience that at the core of what we take for graceful, contemporary living is a poverty and an ugliness born of deceit, and this must be done in theatrical terms, so that it is not unbearable to view for the whole evening. It should be an artistic and satirical interpretation of what is garish and ugly, and consequently not garish and ugly in itself. As with the acting, the decor should be "put on" rather than "be".

As a practical suggestion, I strongly recommend the designer to think first of the colour scheme, as this is probably the most significant contribution to the post-war semi-detached style. Two-tone is the order of the day. If two complementary colours are chosen and emphasized throughout the decor, it will give the effect of lively antagonism and garishness while not displeasing the spectator. The most outrageous of these combinations I feel to be yellow and violet. If the three-piece suite is made of violet plastic material, the two interior walls to the left and the right of the stage can be of the same colour in a lighter or darker tone. To contrast with these the back wall can have a bold contemporary wall-paper of a leaf or cane design stressing a jungle effect in the complementary colour of yellow with its adjacent colours of yellow-orange and yellow-green. The two flush doors can be painted yellow and violet respectively. The flimsy contemporary bookshelves and sideboard can be orange in colour, suggesting that they are made of a plastic imitation of wood.

The form of the total construction will depend upon the size of the stage but ideally, whatever the available space may be, it should present a satirical comment or a caricature. With the larger stage, a skeleton structure of the whole house can be shown, using thin laths of wood or even wire to indicate the flimsiness of the fabric. If the room itself is stylized with pictures, mirrors and perhaps furniture painted on the walls, the car should be a "cut-out", stressing the "sheerline" approach to modern motor manufacture. The railway should be built on supports as, in practice, this makes Fred's entrance more absurd than if he were crouching on the ground. It enables him to alight from his trolley as swiftly and nimbly as if he were on a bicycle and this joke is certainly heightened by being performed rapidly.

On a smaller stage, the external parts of the house can be omitted, together with the car and the railway. If also the stage has a low proscenium and the structural aspects of the house cannot be shown, it will mean that the full caricature must be revealed in the room itself. In which case, I recommend a highly stylized set, the walls of the room appearing as a triptych against dark curtains or a subdued cyclorama. In whatever way the set is built, the audience must feel that it is removed from naturalism.

The Direction

A classical satire on our contemporary scene together with its appropriate presentation is unusual in our modern English drama. The style is characterized by unity, economy and a clear, balanced pattern. In a sense, the unity is derived from the dialogue, characterization, plot, acting, movement and setting all appearing larger than life. But this effect is produced not necessarily by overplaying but by limiting the range of the audience's thought to a series of essential images which jointly represent the absurdity of Man in his modern culture.

The audience should also feel that it is a bold statement of essential, comic theatre, a hilarious romp, an evening of fun which is being shared with the actors. It was first written for a cathedral festival and should be an open, gay, communal admission of our follies.

One last pitfall which I feel I should mention. Some producers may know that I was born in Birmingham. Consequently it may be thought that the play should be presented in a Birmingham accent. This can be disastrous. To insist upon a detailed, authentic, regional accent suggests a naturalistic approach which is alien to the Classical style of the play. This script does not ask the audience to recognize and come to terms with the author's world but with its own. Therefore, the play should be performed in those accents which cause the audience to make this response.

The satire, as far as accent is concerned, lies in the general belief that cultured speech is a prerequisite for social advancement. Fred and Hilda, therefore, have adopted speech characteristics which try to hide their humble origins and give an appearance of refinement. A requirement of the acting is exaggeration, and so the effect should be one of highly genteel articulation with an underlying vulgarity.

The audience should not be conscious of any particular regional accent but only of a powerful attempt to conceal one. Perhaps the best way of doing this is for the actor to take the local accent of the audience and distort it into refined speech by turning the vowels into "posh" diphthongs and by overstressing the consonants. In which case, Avril, Tom and Eileen will have an accent which corresponds more closely to that of the area in which the play is presented. Their speech is not as self-conscious as that of their parents.

DAVID TURNER

Semi-Detached

The play was commissioned by the Belgrade Theatre, Coventry, and first presented in June, 1962, as part of the Festival to celebrate the reopening of Coventry Cathedral. It had the following cast:

HILDA MIDWAY	.. ..	.. Gillian Raine
FRED MIDWAY	.. ..	.. Leonard Rossiter
TOM MIDWAY	.. ..	.. Ian McKellen
EILEEN MIDWAY	.. ..	.. Fiona Duncan
ROBERT FREEMAN	.. ..	.. William Holmes
AVRIL HADFIELD	.. ..	.. Bridget Turner
NIGEL HADFIELD	.. ..	Michael Rothwell
GARNET HADFIELD	.. ..	Sheila Keith
ARNOLD MAKEPIECE	.. ..	Brendan Barry

Directed by ANTHONY RICHARDSON with settings by KENNETH BRIDGEMAN

The Publishers are indebted to the Belgrade Theatre, Coventry, for their help throughout the preparation of this edition and, in particular, for the frontispiece and property list.

The play was subsequently produced in London at the Saville Theatre by Oscar Lewenstein, L.O.P. Ltd. and Donald Albery in December, 1962, with the following cast:

FRED MIDWAY	.. ..	.. Laurence Olivier
HILDA MIDWAY	.. ..	Mona Washbourne
TOM MIDWAY	.. ..	.. James Bolam
EILEEN MIDWAY	.. ..	Eileen Atkins
ROBERT FREEMAN	.. ..	John Thaw
AVRIL HADFIELD	.. ..	.. Patsy Rowlands
NIGEL HADFIELD	.. ..	Kenneth Fortescue
GARNET HADFIELD	.. ..	Joan Young
ARNOLD MAKEPIECE	.. ..	Newton Blick

Directed by TONY RICHARDSON with settings by LOUDON SAINTHILL

The action of this play is continuous and takes place in the sitting-room of Fred Midway's house one Sunday morning in the spring.

Running time, excluding intervals, is approximately two hours and ten minutes.

No character in this play is intended to portray any specific person, alive or dead.

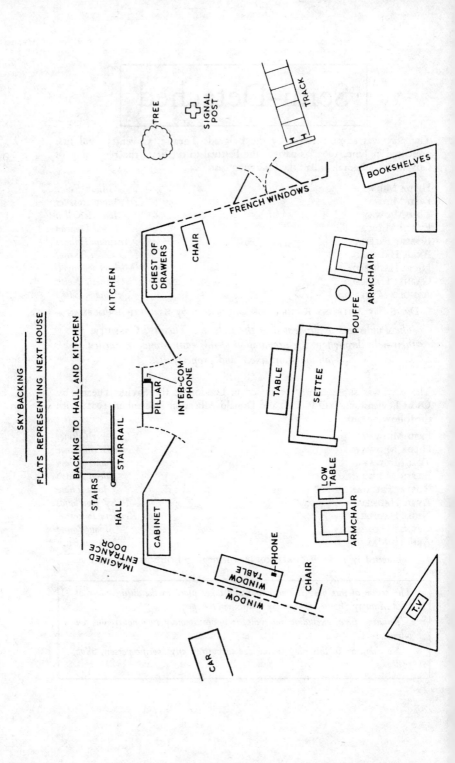

SEMI-DETACHED *

ACT ONE

A section of a semi-detached property at 12 Woody Lane, Dowlihull.
C. stage there is a "through-lounge" with two doors in the back wall, one leading to the hall, the other to the "kitchen-dinette". To the R. of the room are modern square bay windows; to the L. is the french window.
On stage R. is the front lawn and drive. There is an imaginary garage behind the house backstage R. (If the designer wishes, this can be indicated by having an open garage door with a car tyre hanging on it jutting on to the drive.) A car is in the drive.
On stage L. is the rear garden. A fence, partly concealed by flowering shrubs, marks a boundary of the property. The terminus and signal of a small-gauge model railway are near the french windows.

 HILDA, *the mother, is dusting as the curtain rises. She is about forty-eight and wears a skirt and blouse, covered by a pinafore.*
 She moves into the kitchen.
 FRED, *the father, emerges from the garage. He is about fifty and wears slacks, a soft shirt and a yellow woollen cardigan. He is carrying an oil can and dragging a lawn mower which he places on the lawn. He stoops to oil the machine.*
 TOM, *his son, walks slowly along the front garden path. He is nineteen. He is dressed in jeans, a soft shirt and a lightweight sweater. He holds several Sunday newspapers. Oblivious of* FRED, *he is grinning at a picture in one of them.*
 TOM *enters the house, moves through the hall into the room and sits on the settee* C. *He continues to study the picture.*
 FRED, *however, has decided to follow him.*

FRED. Would you please remember I've got a position to keep up?
TOM. Eh?
FRED. When you fetch the Sunday newspapers, carry them neatly tucked underneath your armpit—with the respectable one on the outside. Got it?
TOM. Sorry, Dad. I forgot.
FRED. You've no right to forget. What if, come tomorrow, I say to

---

 * N.B. Paragraph 3 on page 2 of this Acting Edition regarding photocopying and video-recording should be carefully read.

one of my clients, "Jolly thoughtful article in the Magazine Section, wasn't there?"—and he'd seen you smirking the length of our road at a pin-up girl?

Tom. She isn't bad, though, is she, Dad?

Fred (*glancing at the paper*). Very eager and frolicsome, I've no doubt. But I will not allow this young lady's contours and my public face to come together. (*Pause. Moving to* R.C. *front.*) I'm getting a bit cheesed with your basic, elementary pubescence and I don't mind saying it.

Tom. You're what?

Fred. That new motor-bike outside! I suppose you got your mother to sign the H.P. form, is that it?

Tom. That's it.

Fred. I had hoped you'd grown out of motor-bikes. Trying to do on two wheels what a grown man does on four—most adolescent!

    (Hilda *enters from the kitchen, carrying a vase of flowers, which she takes to the front window-sill,* R.)

Hilda. Oh, it's only you, Tom. I heard the conflab, so I thought our Eileen must have come back.

Fred. No, Mother. They haven't arrived yet.

Hilda (*while making a final arrangement to the flowers*). "They"? Who's the "they"? Let's hope there's no "they" about it.

Fred. There's no what?

Hilda. I've given her strict instructions she's not to dare come back up our garden path—not in the company of Bob.

Fred (*worried*). You haven't told Bob to stay away? (*Rising.*) Here, Mother! What have you done?

Hilda. I impressed upon her that they're not to come back together.

    (*This remark takes* Fred's *breath away.* Hilda *doesn't realize this as she has her back towards him while still arranging the flowers on the window-ledge.*)

You know, there are only three houses along here with flowers in the window.

Fred (*moving to her,* R.). Hilda—

Hilda (*continuing*). I always say little girls-pulling-their-frocks-out and Alsatian dogs is one thing, but flowers is a different kettle of fish altogether.

Fred (*patiently*). Is Bob coming back with our Eileen or isn't he?

Hilda (*not listening to him. She continues arranging the flowers*). You can tell about folks if they've got flowers in the window. Flowers are always dying and you're always replacing them. That's the beauty of flowers. (*Turns.*) It shows, you know.

FRED. A little less of you floral opulence, Mother—and answer my question.

HILDA (*blankly*). What question?

FRED (*sarcastically*). What question? (*To* TOM. *Looking for support, putting his hand on his son's shoulder.*) Did you hear me ask your mother a question?

TOM (*looking up from the paper. Surprised*). Me?

FRED (*winces*). Get back to your Fleet Street harem, lad.

HILDA. You want to know if Bob's coming?

FRED. Well done, Mother.

> (*During the following* HILDA *takes a duster from her pocket and moves* D.L., *doing odd spots of polishing.*)

HILDA. Of course he's coming. Only I gave our Eileen a very strict talking-to before she went away.

FRED. You did?

HILDA. I said, "We don't mind your going for a week's holiday with your young man—not in the least. We only hope it might bear fruit, and you'll come home all radiant and engaged. But whatever happens, we mustn't let the neighbours smell out an inkling, must we?"

FRED (*impressed and backing her up*). Certainly not!

HILDA. So whatever they've been doing together, Father, I've impressed upon her to return separate. Is that sensible or isn't it?

FRED. Most sensible, Mother!

> (*During the following* HILDA *picks up a crumb tray and brush from the table and goes to sweep the carpet in front of chair* L. *where* FRED *has left a trace of ash.*)

HILDA. I put it to her, "Your father's an area supervisor. He's not a common or garden insurance man, not now. (*Stooping.*) He's an area supervisor. (*Rising.*) So whatever you do, do it careful."

FRED (*moving* D.R.). Don't discourage her though, love. Don't discourage her. That young man of hers is very useful to me.

HILDA (*while plumping the cushion on chair* L.). I know he is. And it's only to be hoped, after a week at Bournemouth, she's put herself in a much more satisfactory position with him. (*She moves towards the kitchen as if to leave, but* TOM's *trousers catch her eye. She stops.*) You didn't, did you?

TOM. Didn't what?

HILDA (*moving to* L. *side of settee*). You didn't go into Dowlihull to fetch the newspapers—not in those trousers?

TOM. Why?

HILDA. You mean to say you actually walked along the Dowlihull

High Street on a Sunday morning dressed like that?

TOM. What's wrong, Mom?

HILDA. If there's anybody going to let us down in this family, it'll be him. You deal with him, Father.

FRED (*smiles and moves to* R. *side of settee*). Now, now, Mother. Nothing to get upset about. Funny, isn't it, how we hang on to certain working-class habits even though we've improved upon ourselves.

HILDA (*to* TOM). Did you hear what your father said? You're lowering us.

FRED. Correction, Mother, if you don't mind.

HILDA. What?

FRED. I wasn't referring to *his* working-class habits. I was referring to *yours*. Just a mere minor *faux pas* in your social orientation, Mother.

HILDA (*moving* R. *round the back of the settee and joining Fred*). Here! What are you on about? Are you suggesting I've got working-class habits? I've never been afflicted that way—never! Not even when we lived at five back of twenty-two.

FRED. I'm only trying to point out that the wearing of a best suit early on a Sunday morning is very proletariat nowadays and labels one as such.

HILDA. Oh, it does, does it?

FRED (*airily moving* D.L.). You don't go out on a Sunday morning, love—so you wouldn't know.

HILDA. How should he be dressed, then?

FRED (*now* D.L. *Said outwards to audience*). Up till eleven o'clock a somewhat baggy, jumpery, matey look is most *de rigueur*.

HILDA (*perplexed*). It is?

FRED (*nods*). Quite definitely. It suggests you've got a new car to take care of and you've been washing it— (*To* TOM.) That's a hint, lad. Time you got polishing the car, it's your Sunday stint.

TOM. All right. I will in a tick.

FRED (*moving to* R. *of settee and referring to the paper*). Can't you drag yourself away from it? (*Looking at the paper over* TOM'S *shoulder.*) Oh dear! My son!

TOM. I'm looking for what type my next girl friend's going to be.

FRED. What happened to your last one, then? Three weeks ago you were all hot under the collar.

TOM. She took a fancy to somebody else.

HILDA (*to* TOM). She did? Well, we're pleased to hear it. (*To* FRED.) He never brought her round here, you know—he never showed her to us. So we know what kind of a girl she was.

TOM. Mother, she's finished with. (*Referring to the paper.*) I'm picking myself another.

HILDA (*ploughing on with her thoughts, moving* D.R.). When a young lad comes home at night looking as worried as you have—telling us about a young lady he's found with one breath and talking about emigrating with another—we can put two and two together. (*To* FRED.) I do wish you'd have a nice talk with him.

FRED. As I see it, Mother, he's in dire need of a physical outlet. (*To* TOM) Go on! Get out there and start sublimating.

TOM. Eh?

FRED. The car wants cleaning. So stop gawping at that lot and get your hands round my headlamps. (*Snatching the paper and hitting* TOM *with it, he forces him to the hall door.*) Go on! Jildy! Get those hormones into line! (*He closes the door on him.*)

(*After a moment,* TOM *appears through the front door and starts cleaning the car.*)

(*Moving* D.L.) There y'are, Mother. How's that for mind over matter?

HILDA (*moving* U.R., *she empties an ash tray into the crumb tray*). You're clever at it, Dad. When you switch on your talk you can't help but command respect. Well, you always baffle 'em with your knowledge, don't you?

FRED (*referring admiringly to his encyclopedias and touching them*). I've never let dust settle on my encyclopedias, Mother—Many's the night I've spent with you, my beauties! I've done you from cover to cover! The little seducers have lifted the veils all right. Talk about the tree of knowledge! They show you everything bar the forbidden fruit.

HILDA. Forbidden fruit?

FRED. How to make the money! No, love, these are the lads for that. My correspondence courses! And how are you doing down there?

(*He opens the bottom of the cupboard. He takes out several of the files at random. First a large, bound book file.*) "Dynamic Word Power"— (*An even larger bound book file.*) "Psychology and Salesmanship"— (*An enormous bound book file.*) "Promotion Awaits You"— (*Flipping the pages.*) This is the one with that beautiful essay on "How To Destroy Your Colleagues' Self-Confidence"—What's this? (*He removes a slim disc jacket of the talking book type.*) "The Achievements of Western Civilization" on a forty-five r.p.m. Marvellous! (*He puts the files and the record back while he is talking.*) All the same, my view is: it's no use having the polish unless you know how to sell it.

HILDA. That's how you put us where we are, love—chatting to your clients about their interests.

FRED (*sits on settee*). Oh yes, I must say of late I've got myself very gifted in communication. It isn't simply insurance policies I deal in, but gentle and sympathetic understanding.

HILDA (*joins him on the settee*). I can just imagine you doing it.

FRED. Well, it's basic to life, Mother—Know your neighbour's needs! Form an affinity with him! Let there be fellowship, harmony and trust between you! Then take out your catalogue and get flogging!

HILDA. Just to think you started off like anybody else. Going round on your bike—collecting their tenpence a week.

FRED (*nostalgically*). Oh, yes. Those old fifty-quid policies—just for the hearse and the funeral clothes.

HILDA. You've progressed, Fred. (*Sentimentally.*) I always think the turning-point was when we got this house.

FRED. Our little semi?

HILDA. Fred?

FRED. Yes, love?

HILDA. Why do you always call it a semi—and not a house?

FRED. 'cos we're only half-way there, love—half-way to our goal. (*Rising.*) One day, I'd like us to be completely detached.

HILDA. Detached?

FRED (*moving to french window and looking out*). That's what I'm striving for, Mother. Whether we get there or not is a different matter, though.

HILDA. You could do anything you set your mind to. I've got faith in you.

FRED (*turns towards her. Wistfully*). Have you, love?

HILDA (*biting her lip. Emotionally towards audience*). Faith! If you say you'll do it, you'll do it.

FRED. Perhaps you're right. Now I'm a member of the Dowlihull Locomotive Engineers, I think I might have my first foot on the heights.

HILDA. It's only the cream of the cream in the Railway Club. It's noted for that.

FRED. It isn't just the status appeal, you know. There's a lot of business attached.

HILDA. I knew it wouldn't be all pleasure with you—nothing ever is.

FRED (*moving D.L. a little*). Naturally. I mean, it's all a matter of who you know if you don't happen to be born into it. That's why I've always striven very hard with my community life. Remember how when we first came out here I joined the Literary Group? (*Laughs.*)

Oh dear! I didn't flog many policies to them, did I? All very poetic and impecunious, that lot!

HILDA. You didn't see much of 'em, though, Fred—not after you joined the Golf Club.

FRED (*musing. Moving behind the settee to the front window* R.). The Golf Club—fifty quid that cost me for the tackle alone—but it was worth it. I sold many an endowment policy, you know, round about the eleventh hole.

HILDA. The eleventh hole?

FRED. That's when the resistance is low and they feel a long way from home— But I don't think you can top the Loco Club—not unless you've got your own yacht or something. (*Moving to the french windows.*) My little workshop down the garden might not be much to look at, but d'you know the price of the machinery in it?

HILDA. A good bit, I bet.

FRED. Fifteen hundred quid wouldn't touch it.

HILDA. As much as that?

FRED. The lathe alone 'ud cost three-fifty—then I've got my millers and drillers and grinders.

HILDA. And all for free.

FRED. Well, no. Not exactly free. Bob's sort of fiddled them for me out of the firm's store-room—on permanent loan, as you might say.

HILDA (*moving to* R. *of settee*). The day Eileen brought Bob home I knew it'd be a blessing.

FRED. I never even dreamt I could achieve the steam locomotive class, Hilda—not me. It's a rich man's hobby, that—it's only for lawyers and butchers and estate agents and such-like.

HILDA. And you're rubbing shoulders with them now!

FRED. It must be fate! Our Eileen brings home the manager of the Lightcraft Engineering Company. She gets the romance—and I get the tools!

HILDA. We couldn't refuse him, could we?

FRED. Refuse him?

HILDA. Him taking her to Bournemouth.

FRED (*joining* HILDA *in front of settee and holding her hands*). Mother! What are you talking about? I put it in his head to ask her.

HILDA. You did what?

FRED. I put it to him that as their holidays coincided, nobody would object if he wanted to get to know my daughter at—a bit closer range.

HILDA. You actually said that to him?

FRED. I assure you, Hilda—there was nothing direct and sordid in my words. No, I left it all very vague and implicit.

HILDA. No—I'm only amazed, love, 'cos I put the same idea to Eileen.

FRED. You did? That's touching—husband and wife with one aim in mind.

(*They embrace.*)

HILDA (*parting and moving* D.C. *towards audience*). Why couldn't they think of it themselves? It's not like our Eileen to be shy.

FRED. Eileen worries me sometimes.

HILDA. Me, too.

FRED (*moving to join* HILDA D.C.). We've tried to bring her up respectable—and look at her: cram-full! of left-wing drivel about honesty and integrity. (*He bites his lip in sorrow.*)

HILDA (*sorrowing as if her daughter had fallen*). What's got into her, Fred? What's made her that way?

(*The pair of them are now standing front* C. *stage, giving an almost sentimental patter act to the audience.*)

FRED. I think she hates her dad—She says I belong to the corrupt generation.

HILDA. Now, Fred, don't be silly. You're always at loggerheads—but in her heart she worships you.

FRED (*sincerely*). Does she?

HILDA. You're very fond of her, aren't you?

FRED. Yes, Mother. She's our first-born. She brought us together.

HILDA (*almost sighs*). Yes—yes, she did. (*Pause.*) Fred?

FRED. Yes?

HILDA. I sometimes think she's different 'cos she wasn't born out here. Our other two have known decent going-on from their first breath.

FRED. True.

HILDA. Eileen spent the first seven years of her life with us in Piggott Street. I think it might have left an impression.

FRED. Yes, you might be right. It's her formative years on the bubble —Her psychology's still giving her what for.

HILDA. You think so?

FRED (*moving to front window* R.). It's a noted fact. The Jesuits once said, "Give us a child till he's seven and we'll guarantee he'll be done for".

HILDA. "Jesuits"? Who's the Jesuits?

FRED (*indicating encyclopedias*). They're in Volume J, Mother.

(TOM *is about to enter the garage.* FRED *opens the window and calls out to him.*)

Where are you off to now?

Tom. I'll clean my motor-bike now I've got the polish out.
Fred. Don't waste it! Ten bob a tin!
(Tom *enters the garage.* Hilda *joins* Fred *at the window.*)
Hilda. You haven't done the lawn yet.
Fred. I've got the tackle out to show willing.
Hilda. The lawn's got to be done, though. We've left it a week and we don't want no comparisons made—not with next door.
Fred. Comparisons made? Us with next door? You only have to look at the drive to know what class they are. Look at it! Concrete. Self-mix. Three week-ends he laboured on that—and it's cracking already.
Hilda. Mmm. I'm glad you insisted on the red drive. It cost money but it's the only one in the road—that's how I look at it.
Fred (*nods*). I said to the manager of the firm who laid it, "I want it to be the exact colour of that load they've got in front of Buckingham Palace". 'cos none of us knows our potential, do we?
Hilda. You will do the lawn, though?
(*During the following* Eileen, *aged twenty-nine, walks up the front path into the house. She wears a raincoat and carries a suitcase.*)
Fred. Mother, I'll do the lawn! But my King George the Fifth has got to be seen to first. It's got a sticking piston. As soon as it gets its steam up, it does nothing but dribble. (*He glances through the window.*) Look out—it's her!
Hilda. Eileen? (Fred *nods.*) Is Bob with her? (Fred *shakes his head.*) That's nice. She's showed her discretion, then.
(Hilda *moves into the hall to welcome and embrace* Eileen. Fred *moves across stage to* D.L. *Off stage we hear:*)
(*Off.*) Eileen! Come back to a girl's best friend, have you?
Eileen (*off*). Hello, Mom.
Hilda. Your Daddy's in the through-lounge. (*They enter.*) Can you spare him a kiss or do you think you'll be robbing your Bobby?
Eileen (*crossing to* Fred *and giving him a perfunctory kiss*). Hello, Dad.
Hilda (*moving* D.R.). Had a good time, have you?
Eileen (*moving to* C.). Fine.
(*During the following,* Eileen *removes her gloves and raincoat. She is wearing a severe dress. Her shoes are "sensible".*)
Hilda. Weather been nice?
Eileen. Lovely.
Hilda. We had your card with the seagulls.
Eileen. Good.
Hilda. And your father had one from Bob, didn't you, Dad? Ooh, a very naughty p.c. that was—I said to your dad, "What's he been

up to?"—'cos I never knew he had thoughts like that in his head.

FRED (*moving* U.L. *to french windows*). How long before Bob gets here, Eileen?

EILEEN. Ten minutes. Why?

FRED. Well, he'll be anxious to get started on the locos, won't he?

EILEEN (*firmly*). On no, he won't.

FRED. What d'you mean, "Oh no, he won't"? He's my fireman. He's going up to the club track with me this afternoon.

EILEEN. Not if I can help it.

FRED. Oh dear, she's back. Nothing but contradict.

EILEEN. He's not going up that club track this afternoon or any afternoon in future.

FRED. Indeed?

EILEEN. A whole week and he's talked about nothing but Puffer Billies.

FRED (*amazed, moving* D.L.). Puffer Billies? Mother, she can't be talking about my scale-model, precision-built steam locomotives, can she?

HILDA (*moving in between* EILEEN *and* FRED *and then leading him to french window*). Now, now, you two! The minute you're together again there's nothing but ructions! Dad, you'd better get down to your shed. (*Coyly.*) Mother wants a little *tête-a-tête* with her daughter in any case.

FRED. Oh, very well. (*Moves through french windows.*) Send Bob down as soon as he arrives.

EILEEN (*sitting in chair* R. *and calling*). You'll be lucky!

(FRED *leaves.* HILDA *moves to* EILEEN.)

HILDA. I wish you wouldn't aggravate your father, I really do.

EILEEN. Bob's being brain-washed by him. D'you know that? He's talked railways till I'm sick.

HILDA. You've done other little things besides chat, I know—When will he be popping it on your third-finger-left hand, then?

EILEEN. When will he be what?

HILDA. I know what it is! You're not wearing the ring yet, 'cos you've made up your minds to have a proper engagement party!

EILEEN. What are you talking about, Mother?

HILDA. Tell me, love. You've come back on a different footing with him— You must have!

EILEEN. Different footing?

HILDA. Eileen, love! I know you've got generous inclinations—but there are some things a man must pay for!

EILEEN. Mother! What Bob and I have been doing this last week is entirely our business.

HILDA. Naturally it is, love. I'm not one to pry into the intimacies.
I'm only asking, "What have you got to show for it"?

EILEEN. If this is what I've come home to, I wish I'd never come
back.

HILDA. Eileen! We're only thinking of your future. I mean, to put it
frankly, you wouldn't say yourself you're still a Dowlihull deb—
would you?

EILEEN. Mother!

HILDA. Your sister married when she was only nineteen.

EILEEN. What of it?

HILDA. Only that it might reflect on you, love—and we don't want
you labelled. I mean, our Avril happens to be seven years your
junior—She's happily settled and everybody knows it.

EILEEN (sarcastically). Oh, yes. It was a beautiful match, Mother.

HILDA (sitting on settee). Well, it was! What! With his uncle owning
the button factory, Nigel's in direct line for it—don't you forget
that.

EILEEN. I'm hardly likely to.

HILDA. Well, we couldn't hold our Avril back when she had a chance
like that.

EILEEN. Hold her back? Dad couldn't have clapped 'em closer together if he'd used Bostik!

HILDA. Opportunity doesn't knock twice, love—and me and your
dad was only thinking about her interests.

EILEEN. Not just hers, Mother. Dad hasn't done so badly out of it.

HILDA. He's never got anything direct and financial out of it— Just
the mention that we're now allied to the Makepieces adds a bit of
trimming to his status, that's all.

EILEEN. Is that all? I thought he'd managed to squeeze our Tom into
the button works.

HILDA. Oh well, he did do that for the lad, I must admit. But he's
only a managerial apprentice, you know.

EILEEN (rising and going to the table behind the settee for a cigarette which
she lights). Give him a chance, Mother. You can't expect to see him
on the board of directors—not yet.

HILDA. Now don't sound so spiteful. Your father's only got the
interests of the family at heart. He loves his family—he worships it.

EILEEN. He also thinks a family that prays together, stays together.

HILDA (moved). I'm glad you've said that, Eileen. There's a very high-
minded, spiritual side to him as well, you know.

EILEEN. He spells it P R E Y.

HILDA (*rising*). What a thing to say, our Eileen! What a terrible thing
to say! I hope you never let thoughts like that get beyond these
four walls— (*Changes and walks* D.S. *to audience.*) Oh dear, oh dear!

EILEEN. What is it? I've upset you?

HILDA. No, no—it isn't that. Prayers has reminded me. It's the first
Sunday in the month, isn't it?

EILEEN (*moving* D.L.). Yes. Why?

HILDA. It's thinking so much about you—it's gone clean out of my
mind.

EILEEN. What has?

HILDA. Your sister will be turning up soon with her hubby.

EILEEN. On their way back from church?

HILDA. I think our Avril's managed that nicely, don't you? She knew
Nigel was a bit on the religious side when she married him. She
told him flat. If they went to church every week people might
think they were a bit peculiar along their road. But once a month
is sort of tasteful. (*Taking the newspapers and putting them on the table
behind the settee.*) There's something very respectable about once
a month.
   (*During the above* TOM *has wheeled his bike out of the garage
   and into the drive.*)

EILEEN (*nods*). They can take in the Lord Almighty and our little lot
in one journey.

HILDA. Eileen! You haven't turned atheist on top!

EILEEN (*moving to hall door*). I'd better change—tell me when Bob
arrives. (*She leaves.*)
   (HILDA *moves to the window.*)

HILDA. Thomas!

TOM. What is it?

HILDA. I'd like a word with you.

TOM. Well?

HILDA. We'll have no discussions in public, if you don't mind. Inside!
   (TOM *enters the house.* HILDA *moves* D.L., TOM *to* D.C.)
I want you to go and put your trousers on.

TOM. I've got my trousers on.

HILDA. You know what I mean—your Sunday-best trousers.

TOM. But you heard what Dad said—

HILDA. I know what your dad said—but it happens to be the first
Sunday in the month—and you know what that means.

TOM. Oh, they're coming, are they?

HILDA. Yes, they are—and you know how toney Nigel always looks
—hand sewn from head to foot. Go and put your rigout on, there's

a good lad, just to please me.

TOM. Okee-doke. I'm easy.

(*During the above* BOB, *aged thirty, has walked along the drive and he now rings the chimes. He is dressed in flannel trousers and a blazer, with a scarf tucked in an open-necked shirt.*)

HILDA. There's Bob. Tell him to come in.

(TOM *leaves into the hall.* HILDA *moves* U.L.)

TOM (*off*). Come on in, Bob.

BOB (*off*). A new bike, I see.

TOM (*off*). Ah. A smasher. Does the ton.

BOB (*off*). I bet.

(BOB *enters.*)

HILDA (*coldly*). Good morning, Robert.

BOB (*moving* D.C.). Good morning, Mrs. Midway.

HILDA. You've had a very nice week with my daughter, no doubt.

BOB. Very nice, Mrs. Midway—very nice.

HILDA. Well, I'm not going to beat about the bush, Robert. I'm going to put it to you straight.

BOB. Put what?

HILDA. It's very simple, to my mind— Are you going to do the honourable thing by her or aren't you?

(FRED *arrives urgently through the french windows. He has come back to collect some large blueprints of locomotive designs from a shelf* D.R.)

FRED (*crossing the stage rapidly*). Bob, you're here! (*Sorting out the blueprints.*) Why didn't you tell me he was here, Mother? What do you think I bought my inter-com. for?

HILDA (*crossing to* FRED D.R.). He's only just arrived.

FRED (*having opened a blueprint, he is studying it*). Well, you'd better come down the shed. It's urgent.

BOB. Certainly.

(FRED *moves to the french window.* BOB *follows.*)

HILDA. Dad!

FRED. What?

HILDA. Our Eileen's come back—and she hasn't changed her position in life.

FRED. Mother! Don't pester him—there's a crisis on down in that shed.

HILDA. But he hasn't done the honourable thing!

FRED. What does honour matter when my King George the Fifth has got a sluggish injector?

BOB (*anxiously*). It hasn't?

FRED. It has!

HILDA (*moving to* C. *stage*). You must talk over our Eileen—you must! The time's ripe, Father! He's just spent a week with her! He's been enjoying the fruits!

FRED (*angry. Joining* HILDA C. *stage*). Mother! This is not the moment for your bedtime stories!

HILDA. What do you mean?

FRED. I've just told you. I've got an obstruction in my injector system. I'm going to look a real fool up that track this afternoon.

BOB (*coming* D.L.). Have you tried pinching your rubber feed connection while your steam valve's open?

FRED. 'course I have. But instead of having a good blow out through my overflow, it just drips!

HILDA. Aren't you going to discuss Eileen, then?

FRED. Where's your tact, Hilda? I shall be needing every ounce of this lad's ingenuity if I'm going to get my 4–6–0 up that track! He's got no time for sexual post-mortems.

HILDA. Well, if you're not all that concerned about your daughter, I don't see why I should be.

FRED (*ushering her into the kitchen*). That's the spirit, Mother. Get him a cup of tea! We don't want him any more exhausted than what he's come back.

HILDA. Right you are, love. I know how important he is to you. (*To* BOB, *trying to make amends.*) Would you like a Pelican Choc Bar with your tea—

BOB. Thanks, Mrs. Midway.

HILDA. —or would you rather have a Dairy Crackle Finger? They came out last week on the telly.

BOB. Very nice.

HILDA (*at the kitchen door*). Which do you want, then? A Pelican Choc—or a Dairy Crackle Finger?

FRED. Give him both, Mother. It'll help to build him up.

(HILDA *leaves.* FRED *makes for the french windows.* BOB *doesn't appear to wish to leave. He has something on his mind and wanders* C. *stage.*)
(*At french windows.*) Coming?

BOB. Mr. Midway!

FRED. Yes?

BOB. I assure you I love your daughter. It's just that—for various complicated reasons—we can't think of marriage at the moment.

(*The following three pieces of movement by* FRED *are repetitive, mechanical and precise.*)

FRED (*taking two steps towards* BOB). Ah yes—love's always a complicated thing— (*Then making for the french windows again.*) Now about
the obstruction in my outlet valve—

BOB. I think the time has come to be absolutely frank with you and
tell you what prevents our marrying—

FRED (*taking two steps towards* BOB). Another time, perhaps— (*Then
making for the french windows again.*) —but at the moment I've got
an obstruction in my outlet valve.

BOB. There's no one I'd rather live my life with than Eileen; I'd like
you to believe that.

FRED (*taking two steps towards* BOB). Of course I believe you— (*Then
making for the french windows again.*) —but what about the obstruction
in my outlet valve?

BOB. There are certain difficulties.

FRED. There certainly are.

BOB. There's something barring the way.

FRED (*moving to* C. *stage close to* BOB). I know that.

BOB. You know?

FRED. I ought to.

BOB. Eh?

FRED. I've had my drain cocks wide open for the past half-hour with
my pressure right up to danger level. Any more of it and I'll be
straining my boiler in the region of my fire-box. There won't be
much hope then, will there? Well? What do you think?

BOB. You've probably got a leak.

FRED (*rapidly*). Got a leak?

BOB (*rapidly*). In your steam valve duct.

FRED (*rapidly*). In my steam valve duct?

BOB (*rapidly*). That's it.

FRED. You could be right— (*Moving to french windows.*) Come along,
Bob. Let's look at it together. You're my salvation, lad. Come
on— Why are you dawdling about? There isn't much time, if
we're going to get it up that track this afternoon. (*He moves off.*)

(BOB *shrugs his shoulders and follows him.*

HILDA *enters from the kitchen with a tray holding the tea-things.
She puts it down on the small table near the chair* R. *She sits in the
chair and starts pouring tea.*

EILEEN *enters from the hall and crosses* L. *to french windows.*)

EILEEN. Where's Bob?

HILDA. He's gone down to the workshop with your father.

EILEEN (*sarcastically*). Well, that's really marvellous, isn't it?

HILDA. What?

EILEEN. The first minute back and he's commandeered by Dad.

HILDA. Now you know how your father relies on him. It's wonderful the way the pair of them fit in together. Is there a little tray by the sideboard?

EILEEN (*goes to the side of the cabinet* U.L. *and finds it*). This?

HILDA. Let's be having it.

 (EILEEN *comes to* HILDA D.R. HILDA *puts three cups of tea and a plate of biscuits on the small tray.*)

EILEEN. Mother?

HILDA. Yes, love?

EILEEN. I didn't come back to start quarrelling, you know.

HILDA. Let's forget about it, Eileen. (*Pause.*) There are always little problems on a Sunday.

EILEEN. Can I prepare the potatoes or anything?

HILDA. It's going to be a cold lunch—meat and salad. Your dad doesn't like anything big on his stomach up the track.

EILEEN (*wandering to french windows and looking out*). It's a nice day. It's a pity Dad can't take you out for a drive.

HILDA (*wistfully to audience*). Too much traffic nowadays, love. One breath of sun and the country lanes are crowded. All the riff-raff of creation out in their bubble cars. No. If I can have the deck-chair out for an hour by the side of the goldfish pond, that's all I need— Oh, I've just thought— (*Standing.*) One of the goldfish has gone all white and sunk to the bottom. (*Moving to kitchen.*) I'll get a colander so your father can fish him out. (*She goes into the kitchen to fetch a colander. The dialogue continues uninterrupted.*)

EILEEN (*crosses to pick up tray* D.R.). You want me to take these teas down the shed?

HILDA (*off*). Yes, love. One of them's for you.

EILEEN. Thanks. (*She moves towards the french windows round the back of the settee, carrying the tray.*)

 (HILDA *returns with the colander.*)

HILDA. Ask him to bury it down the bottom with Fido.

EILEEN (*takes the colander*). Right you are, Mother.

HILDA. Good.

 (EILEEN *leaves through the french windows.* HILDA *moves to the french windows and says romantically:*)
It's going to be lovely in the garden this afternoon, down by the pool with the Ena Harkness climbing up the trellis. (*To audience as she moves* D.R.) It's a lovely house we've got—whatever Father's ambitions might be. Lovely. (*She sits again* D.R., *sips her tea and eats her biscuit.*)

(*After a moment,* AVRIL, *aged twenty-two, walks up the path and enters the house. She wears a dress and hat, high heels and carries a handbag. She looks smart but cheap, as she chooses clothes that make an obvious impression and advertise her dress allowance. She moves into the through-lounge.*)

AVRIL. Mother!

HILDA. Hello, Avril dear. Church was over early, was it?

(AVRIL *puts her handbag on the table behind the settee.*)

AVRIL. I haven't been.

HILDA. You haven't been? Where's our Nigel, then?

AVRIL (*moving to* D.S. *to* L. *of settee*). He's not coming.

HILDA. Not coming? Has he been took poorly?

AVRIL. No, Mother. He's not poorly.

HILDA. What is he, then, if he's not poorly?

AVRIL. I've left him.

HILDA (*not registering*). You've what?

AVRIL (*moves to* D.C.). I've left him, Mother.

HILDA (*almost casually*). "Left him"? What do you mean . . . "left him"?

AVRIL. It's too terrible to talk about.

HILDA (*alarmed, she shrieks*). Left him?

AVRIL. Yes, Mother, left him.

(*She sobs.*)

HILDA (*moving rapidly to* AVRIL C.). What's he done? What's he done to you, love? Tell your mother now. What's he done?

AVRIL. He's done it across me.

HILDA. Done it across you? You don't mean—

AVRIL. I do.

HILDA. Nigel? Not Nigel?

AVRIL. He's a dirty beast, Mother!

HILDA. Never! Nigel a dirty beast?

AVRIL. He's been with another woman.

HILDA (*hand up to her face in shock. To audience*). No!

AVRIL (*howls*). I tell you he has!

(*Pause.*)

HILDA. Well, I don't know. Nigel, of all people— Who is she?

AVRIL. It's too disgusting.

HILDA. What's her name?

AVRIL. Mother, I don't like shaping the word with my lips!

HILDA. Not one of them! He hasn't been with one of them?

AVRIL. She was a woman of the street—only in a house.

HILDA. Where?

AVRIL. London.

HILDA. London?

AVRIL. He went down there yesterday for the Cup Final.

HILDA. Cup Final?

AVRIL. He went with Tommy Hickerton.

HILDA. Not the Tommy Hickerton down by the garage opposite the bridge?

AVRIL. Yes, that's right.

HILDA. The school teacher?

AVRIL (*she howls, moving* D.S.R.). I thought my Nigel would be safe with a school teacher!

HILDA. Don't say any more! Don't say any more! I want your father to hear every word. (*She moves to the inter-com set fixed to the back wall between the two doors and turns the handle rapidly.*) Dad!— Can you hear me? (*Shouting above his steam-engine noises.*) What's all that row down there?— If I shout, can you hear me?— Come up here quick!— I don't care if you are getting your steam up; come up here quick!— What about? It's Avril. She's—

AVRIL. The neighbours, Mother!

HILDA (*to* AVRIL). You're right. (*Into phone.*) Just come up here! (*She moves to comfort* AVRIL. *Seating* AVRIL *on the settee.*) There now, love—there.

(AVRIL *howls.*)

Shall I get you a cup of tea?

(AVRIL *howls.*)

(*Standing to* R. *of settee.*) How do you know he's misbehaved himself? How do you know?

AVRIL. He told me.

HILDA. He told you? Are you sure he wasn't joking or anything?

AVRIL (*howls*). No!

HILDA. It's most unlike Nigel, I must say— Here, Avril! Perhaps he was boasting. (AVRIL *howls.*) There, love, there. Don't take on, Avril, love. Try to be brave. Me and your father'll get it all sorted out—don't you worry.

(FRED *enters urgently through the french windows.*)

FRED (*standing to* L. *of settee*). Now then, what's all the panic about? (AVRIL *howls.*) What's up with her?

HILDA. Something delicate's happened to her, Dad—something very delicate. Tell him, Avril—tell him.

AVRIL. I can't, Mother.

FRED. What is it?

HILDA. Her Nigel's been unfaithful.

FRED. He's what?

HILDA. He's misbehaved himself.

FRED. Nigel misbehaved himself? You're not having me on, are you?

HILDA. I wish I was— Tell him, Avril.

AVRIL. He's been with one of them women, Dad.

FRED. One of what women?

HILDA. She's just told you.

FRED. You don't mean a—

HILDA. Father!

(AVRIL *howls*.)

FRED (*moving* D.S.L., *laughing and sharing his mirth with the audience*). No— no—never. Not Nigel—no, never. Not him!

HILDA. It's right, Dad.

FRED (*returns to* L. *of settee*). Has she told you how it happened?

HILDA. She said it was in London. He went down for the Cup Tie— with Tommy Hickerton.

FRED. Tommy Hickerton?

AVRIL. Nigel didn't want to go at first. He's not the sporting type, as you know. But I forced him. I said he hung about the house too much—that he ought to have an outside interest. (*Thinking of the irony*.) Outside interest! Ooh, Mother!

FRED (*moving* U.S. *to behind settee*). Now then, Avril. Less of the fairy fountains. Let's have it all in perspective.

HILDA. Let's hear what Nigel said.

FRED. What did he say to you?

AVRIL. He said—

FRED. Yes?

AVRIL. He said after the match was over Tommy Hickerton thought the M1 would be crowded—and you know he's a bit nervous of the M1, is Nigel.

FRED. Go on.

AVRIL. Tommy Hickerton said it would be better if they had a snack somewhere. So he took my Nigel down to Leicester Square.

FRED. Oh he did, did he? And they ended up in one of them streets round the back, did they?

AVRIL. That's right, Dad.

FRED (*moving to* D.S.L.). That's where it all takes place, Mother.

HILDA. How do you know, Dad?

FRED (*returning to* L. *of settee*). I read the newspapers, don't I? (*To* AVRIL.) Go on, love.

AVRIL. Well, they had some sandwiches and some beer—and you know how he can't stand strong drink.

FRED. Ah. He goes all dopey if he has half a shandy.

AVRIL. Anyway, Nigel says they were trying to find where they'd parked the car when Tommy Hickerton was lured up some stairs by a woman in a doorway.

HILDA. And what did Nigel do?

AVRIL. He followed.

HILDA. Followed?

AVRIL. Yes, Mom, followed.

HILDA. Go on, Avril. What happened?

AVRIL. Well, Nigel went up these stairs and there was another woman at the top— And Tommy Hickerton went into a room with one of them—and Nigel followed suit with the other.

HILDA (*sitting on settee on* AVRIL'S R. *Anxiously*). He did? And what happened?

AVRIL. What happened?

HILDA. Yes, love. What happened?

AVRIL. He succumbed.

HILDA. What d'you mean by "succumbed"?

FRED. What do you think she means by "succumbed"?

(FRED *paces* D.S.L.)

HILDA. So he succumbed, did he?

AVRIL. Yes, Mom.

HILDA. Well, that's that, then. If he succumbed, he succumbed.

FRED (*returning to* L. *of settee*). Wait till I get hold of him— I'll blinkin' succumb him!

AVRIL. When I woke up this morning I found him all stretched out on the divanette in our through-lounge. I said (*Coyly.*) "What's been keeping my little Niggy away from his slumberland?" Then he came out with it! He couldn't get into bed with me 'cos he was all guilt-ridden! (*She howls.*)

HILDA (*comforting her*). The poor love—the poor little love. (*Rising and moving* U.R.) It's hard for you now, Avril—but you wait till you've gone through the making of it up.

(*During the following* HILDA *and* FRED *pace up and down stage on each side of the seated* AVRIL. *Clearly defined symmetry.*)

FRED (*moving* U.L.). Have him on his knees, Avril—have him licking the carpet.

HILDA (*moving* D.R.). Lead him a dance—you're entitled. There'll be flowers, chocolates, new fur coat—anything you fancy.

FRED (*moving* D.L.). It could be most rewarding, Mother. Most rewarding.

HILDA (*moving* U.R.). Just think out what you want, Avril, and it might help you through your grief. Is there anything you want, Avril—anything special you want?

AVRIL. Yes, Mother, I want—

HILDA (*moving to* R. *of settee and standing still, looking down on* AVRIL). Yes? Yes, Avril?

AVRIL. I want—

FRED (*moving to* L. *of settee and standing still looking down at* AVRIL). Well?

AVRIL (*she looks from one parent to the other and then out front*). I want to divorce him.

HILDA }(*lift their heads, look at each other and exclaim*). Divorce him!
FRED }

FRED. No, no—she doesn't mean it, Mother.

HILDA. 'course she doesn't.

FRED. Give her a cup of tea and she'll get over it. (*He moves* D.L.)
                    (HILDA *scurries to the teapot on small table* R.)

AVRIL. You needn't bother. I know what I'm saying. I want to divorce him.

HILDA (*turning inwards*). It's the shock, that's it.

FRED (*turning inwards*). A terrible shock.

AVRIL (*rises and moves* D.C. *and yells to audience*). I want to divorce him!

HILDA (*moving to* AVRIL). Shh! The neighbours!

FRED (*moving to* AVRIL, *controlling the volume of his voice*). The neighbours, love—the neighbours!

HILDA (*voice controlled*). You must remember the neighbours. Whatever happens, you must remember them.

AVRIL (*yells*). I don't care about the neighbours! I want to divorce him!

HILDA. She's overcome. The poor girl's overcome! (*Dragging her back to the settee.*) Sit down, Avril. Sit down.

FRED (*rapidly moving* R. *to the front window*). I'll shut the window; the sound carries.

                    (HILDA *gets* AVRIL *seated again and then moves to* L. *of settee.*
          FRED *closes the window in panic. Once closed, he waves across the road*
          to a neighbour to assure him that everything is normal.)

HILDA (*to* AVRIL). It must be a terrible blow to a young girl; we understand that, dear.

FRED (*moving to behind settee* R., *hushed*). Say what you like now—but don't raise your voice.

HILDA. We've got to treat her gently, Dad. It's all been the tender years of married bliss for her up to now. It's been a rude awakening for her.

FRED. You're right, love—very rude. I'm not disputing it. Only keep your voice low, will you?

AVRIL (*a slow, loud whisper*). I'm going—to divorce him.

FRED (*smiles and sits on the arm of settee* L.). That's better, love—that's better.

HILDA (*smiles and sits on the arm of the settee* R.). That's right, Avril you've found your self-control. You've got to have self-control, whatever the emergency, haven't you, Dad?

FRED. You're quite right, love, you have.

AVRIL. How long will it take to get my freedom—the filthy beast!

FRED. Now, now, Avril—let's view it dignified, shall we?

HILDA. We mustn't cheapen ourselves, whatever happens.

FRED. Seemliness, that's what's called for.

HILDA. He's made a slip and he must suffer. It's only right—but you don't have to talk about divorce, Avril.

FRED. It's got a stigma, has divorce—a very nasty stigma.

HILDA. People are only too ready to cast slurs on you, you know. There'd be a lot of slurs being cast—for all of us.

FRED. We've built up a good name for ourselves in this district—she mustn't forget that.

HILDA. Think of the family, love. You don't want to drag your father's nose through the mire, do you?

FRED. I don't want to stress the point, our Avril, but it could lead to repercussions for me business-wise—have you thought about that?

AVRIL. But I'm the innocent party, Dad.

HILDA. Yes, she is the innocent party, Dad—we mustn't forget that.

FRED. There's no smoke without fire, remember.

HILDA. Quite right, Dad, quite right. But I was thinking if Avril could get him for cruelty on top, it might not turn out so slurry as you think. There might be a lot of sympathy flying in our direction for adultery with cruelty on top. Do you think we could get him for cruelty on top?

AVRIL. He's too wet, Mother—it wouldn't hold water.

FRED (*explodes and marches* U.S.R.). Mother! You're talking through your hat!

HILDA. I'm what?

FRED (*shouts*). She doesn't want to get divorced!

HILDA (*rises*). Voice, Dad, voice!

FRED (*quietly*). She doesn't want to get divorced.

AVRIL. I do, Dad.

FRED. You don't.

AVRIL (*rises*). I do. (*She moves* D.S.R.)

FRED. Will you stop barging in while I'm talking to your mother?

HILDA. I don't see why she shouldn't if it's cruelty on top.

FRED (*marches across stage to* D.S.C.). Let's get this in perspective. Let's see this as it should be seen, shall we? Our Avril's one of the most envied young ladies in the neighbourhood—am I right or aren't I?

HILDA (*considering and moving to* C. *stage*). Well—yes. Nigel's uncle does own the button factory.

FRED. Exactly. And don't forget he's got the belt, buckle and zip-fastener subsidiaries, as well. Nigel's in direct line for all that.

AVRIL. But, Dad—

FRED. Shut your mouth a minute. (*Walking* U.S. *and round settee to* L. *of it.*) Think of all the sacrifices we made to get her united to one of the Hadfields—and Nigel isn't any common or garden Hadfield. He's the chief Hadfield hope, as you might say.

AVRIL. But, Dad—

FRED (*moving* D.S.L. *between* AVRIL *and* HILDA). I'm talking! Divorce him? She must be out of her mind. (*Crossing in front of* HILDA *to* D.S.L.) Look at the money we wasted when we knew he was interested in her. Posh hairdressers down the High Street twice a week—evening dresses, tennis rackets—and what about your riding habits?

HILDA. Your father spent a lot of money on your riding habits.

FRED. And what about all those society pictures you had in the Dowlihull Weekly News? You only had to sip a cocktail or jump on a horse and there you were—half a page and you dead centre.

HILDA. It's right, Avril.

FRED (*moving* U.S.L.). They even had to move the Dog Lovers' Diary one week to squeeze her in.

HILDA. The Mayor's own granddaughter didn't have a better spread.

FRED (*moving* D.L. *again*). And didn't I pay through the nose for it! We'd only got money to put you there, you know.

HILDA. Your father bled himself dry.

FRED (*moving* U.L. *again*). It was an investment—I said at the time it was an investment. And now she wants to chuck it up!

AVRIL. But, Dad—

FRED (*moving rapidly behind settee to* AVRIL D.R.). Shut up, I've told you! You might want to destroy your life—but don't try and destroy mine. Nigel's uncle is a member of the Council, isn't he? Who's going to get the insurance on all the municipal development that's going up? I'll tell you who's going to get it: me!—acting on behalf of the Sunlight Assurance. I shall be the regional officer after that, Mother.

AVRIL. But, Dad—!

FRED. What do you keep "but-Dadding" about?

AVRIL. Nigel's uncle might not stay on the Council.

FRED (*amazed*). Not stay on the Council? Nigel's uncle? (*Scoffs as he moves across stage* D.L.) He'll be there till he gets his O.B.E. What do you think keeps him, otherwise?

AVRIL. But he's got a mistress.

FRED (D.L. *and out to audience*). Got a mistress? Everybody knows he's got a mistress. He's a very rich man—he's entitled to a mistress.

AVRIL. But it's not his old mistress—it's a new mistress.

FRED (*still smiling out to the audience*). Well, it's an accepted fact he likes a change from time to time.

HILDA (*moving to* C. *between* AVRIL *and* FRED. *Explaining to* AVRIL). Once you get high enough, such things don't matter. It's a different way of life, see.

FRED. That's right, Mother. He's above it all.

AVRIL. But she's a factory girl! A Miss Daphne Dunmore—out of his own works! He found her in his zip-fastener extension!

HILDA. In his what?

AVRIL. Zip-fastener extension! She works on the zip-fasteners, Mom.

FRED. Not so much snobbishness, Avril! Titled ladies have been made out of less.

AVRIL. That's right. He's going to marry her.

FRED (*amazed*). He's what?

HILDA (*amazed*). Marry her!

AVRIL. He's going to marry her.

FRED (*refusing to believe it, he laughs, moving* U.S.R.). No, no, you've got it all wrong.

HILDA. He can't marry her—your Nigel might be cut off if he marries her.

AVRIL. Nigel went for his fortnightly visit last Thursday and his uncle told him.

FRED. He did?

AVRIL. Yes.

FRED (*laughing*). He must have been joking. He was pulling your Nigel's leg, that's what it was.

HILDA. Don't be silly, Avril. Nigel's uncle wouldn't lower himself to marry a factory girl.

AVRIL (*with a confident shrug, she moves* D.S.L.). He would, Mom— 'cos he's put her in the family way.

FRED (*aghast*). Put her in the family way?

AVRIL. Yes, Dad.

FRED (*slaps his forehead and stumbles* D.S. *to between* AVRIL *and* HILDA). What? Without consulting anybody?

HILDA. You know what that means, don't you, Dad?

FRED. I know what it means, all right. I can hardly get my breath back.

HILDA. Nigel will be cut off.

FRED (*in grief he stumbles across stage and moves to* U.R.). Clean cut off.

HILDA (*moving to* AVRIL D.L.). If we'd known this would happen, we'd never have let you marry him. Never!

AVRIL. But that's what I'm saying. I want to unmarry him now.

HILDA. Unmarry him?

FRED (*radiant*). She's got a point—our Avril's got a point.

HILDA (*moving to* C.). Oh no, Dad. I don't like divorce—not unless there's cruelty on top.

AVRIL (*following* HILDA *to* C.). But I'm the innocent party, Mom.

HILDA. I know, love, but there's always a tinge of dishonour about it, to my mind.

FRED (*crossing stage from* U.R. *to* D.L., *passing in front of* AVRIL *and* HILDA). Now, Mother, let's have some balance and common sense. (*Pause.*) It doesn't matter so much about dishonour as long as the money's all right.

HILDA. Money? But he's been cut off.

FRED. I'm taking that into consideration. (*Sitting in chair* D.L.) Now, let's view it all fair and square, if you don't mind. As I see it, our Avril can go on living with him as he is now—and what is he as he stands today? The half-bred son of an Income Tax collector, that's all—or she can demand what's due to her and, to call a spade a spade, look elsewhere!

HILDA (*moving slightly* L. *towards* AVRIL). It wouldn't be too late, our Avril; you've still got a lot of the bloom on you.

AVRIL. Dad!

FRED. Yes, love?

AVRIL. What do you think my dues are?

FRED. Your dues? Well, you'll get your alimony—no question about that. But I think if we play our cards right, you'll also get possession of the bungalow.

AVRIL (*elated*). The bungalow!

HILDA. Oh no, I don't think she'll be as lucky as that.

FRED. What do you mean, Mother? The uncle gave it to the pair of them for a wedding present, didn't he? So Avril's already got half of it before she starts claiming.

HILDA. It's a lovely bungalow, Avril, and you've made it so homely.

FRED. Well, what's she going to do then, Mother?

HILDA. How do you mean, Dad?

FRED. Haven't you been listening? I've been trying to give an unbiased, unprejudiced, two-sided view of the situation, haven't I? Does she divorce him or doesn't she?

HILDA. Well, I didn't understand about the bungalow. I mean, if she's going to get the bungalow, I don't really see there's any point in holding on—talk or no talk—and we are the innocent party, after all.

FRED (*rising and moving* U.S.L.). Well, that's that, then.

AVRIL (*overjoyed*). I can divorce him, then, can I?

HILDA. You've got your parents' blessing, dear.

AVRIL (*emotionally. Moving to* HILDA *and embracing her at* L.C.). Oh, Mother! Mother!

HILDA (*holding her in her arms*). There now, Avril. There now.

AVRIL (*sentimentally*). I love my parents. They're so sympathetic and understanding.

HILDA. You've always got something to fall back on in us.

AVRIL (*she kisses* HILDA). Mom— (HILDA *moves to chair* D.R. *and sits.* AVRIL *moves to her father* U.L. *Emotionally.*) I'd like to kiss you, Dad. (*She kisses him. She moves from him to the table behind the settee, where she finds a box of chocolates, chooses one and starts eating it.* FRED *moves to chair* D.L. *and sits. Girlishly.*) I'm all worked up and excited for the day now—silly of me.

HILDA. What day?

AVRIL. The day of my release, of course. Can you wear what you like in the court?

HILDA. Oh, there are a terrible lot of preparations before the divorce.

AVRIL. I think I'll settle for a nice, quiet divorce, Mother.

HILDA. It'll all be done properly, don't you worry.

AVRIL. It's lovely to have something to look forward to. I feel so much better. Do you think I could have a swill in your kitchen-dinette and put my face on?

HILDA. You do, love, you do. (AVRIL *leaves for the kitchen.*) She mustn't go back under the same roof with him now—not on no account.

FRED. 'course she mustn't.

HILDA. If he can claim he's started up his marital rights again—she won't have a leg to stand on.

(TOM *enters from the hall.*)

TOM. Mom— I wonder if you could mend my best trousers for me.
(*He holds them out to her.*)

HILDA. Don't bother me now. Me and your Dad have got serious things on our minds.

TOM. But, Mom—

FRED (*calmly indicating that they do not wish to be disturbed*). You heard what your mother said.

TOM. Well, where's some needles and cotton, then?

HILDA. If it's a button off, you know where the things are always kept —in the electric sewer in our third bedroom.

TOM (*trying to show her the trousers*). Mom, I wonder if you could—

FRED. You heard what your mother said: don't bother her. Now go on. Get out.

TOM. Okee-doke, then. (*He leaves through the door to the hall.*)
(HILDA *moves to the door after him.*)

FRED. Where are you going?

HILDA (*now U.R. of the settee*). I've suddenly remembered he went out on his new motor-bike in his best trousers yesterday—he might have torn them or something.

FRED. That's your fault, isn't it?

HILDA. My fault?

FRED (*dismissing it*). I really think you might have consulted me before you signed that H.P. form.

HILDA (*moving down to C.*). I didn't sign no form. He told me you did.

FRED. I did? I didn't!

HILDA. Well, who did?

FRED (*rising*). I don't know who did! (*Moving to C. to join* HILDA.) How did he get the money, then? He couldn't have paid cash.

HILDA. Dad! Do you think he stole it?

FRED (*gazing perplexedly towards the audience*). Stole it? Our son— acquiring possessions by the direct method! (*He shakes his head perplexedly and moves to window U.R.*)

HILDA (*still C.*). He's been acting strange lately, Father. I thought he'd placed a young lady in a predicament—well, I did find that passionate letter when I went through his pockets. But it isn't that at all—it's this! We've got to talk to him!

FRED. We can't, Mother. We've got enough on our plates at the moment. Look who's just pulled up over the road.

HILDA (*moving U.R., looking through the window*). It's him! It's Nigel!

FRED. And look—he's brought his mother with him.

HILDA. I suspected this might happen.
(FRED *moves rapidly to the kitchen door.* HILDA *goes to the table*

for the tray containing the tea-things.)

FRED. Avril!

AVRIL *(off)*. Just coming, Dad.

> *(AVRIL enters and FRED stands to her R. near the kitchen door.)*

FRED. Your Nigel's arrived with his mother.

AVRIL. What for?

FRED. To get you back, of course. Now don't forget: you're staying here.

AVRIL. I am?

> *(The kitchen door is partly open and HILDA moves between FRED and AVRIL into the kitchen, carrying the tray.)*

FRED. Naturally. *(Warningly.)* One false move with your physical side now—and you'll land yourself up the creek with him for life. Have you got that?

AVRIL. Yes, Dad.

> *(NIGEL and MRS. HADFIELD have moved up the path. They ring the chimes.*
>
> HILDA *returns from the kitchen.)*

FRED. Fair enough, Mother!

> *(HILDA darts through the hall door. As she closes it behind her, FRED closes the kitchen door simultaneously and then rapidly leads AVRIL to the chair D.L. The speed and precision of the action concerning the doors should produce an absurd and highly comic effect.)*

Leave it all to me—and don't forget that *pro tem* you're very *sub judice.*

AVRIL *(now seated D.L.)*. What does that mean, Dad?

FRED *(now standing to attention at R. of AVRIL's chair and looking towards the audience)*. It means at all costs keep your trap shut!

> *(MRS. HADFIELD, NIGEL and HILDA enter. MRS. HADFIELD is wearing an elegant spring suit. Her accessories have been chosen with taste. NIGEL wears a well-cut, formal grey suit. As HILDA has said, he looks "hand-sewn from head to foot". MRS. HADFIELD is about fifty. Nigel is twenty-five.*
>
> HILDA *moves D.R.* MRS. HADFIELD *moves to R.C.* NIGEL *moves to L.C. In the presence of the HADFIELDS, FRED and HILDA use highly refined and dignified voices.)*

MRS. HADFIELD. I expect you already know the reason for our visit.

HILDA *(smiles slightly. Sarcastically)*. We certainly know the reason for Nigel's visit—we're not so sure about yours, Mrs. Hadfield.

MRS. HADFIELD. Mrs. Midway, my son came round this morning and requested me to accompany him. Isn't that so, Nigel?

NIGEL. Definitely.

MRS. HADFIELD (*smiles, as if making a joke*). Knowing the house he was going to call on, I think he felt he might like a witness. (*With a little laugh.*) I told him it was a very silly idea to have—but he did force me along, didn't you, Nigel?

NIGEL. Definitely.

FRED. Won't you sit down, Mrs. Hadfield?

> (*She sits on* R. *of settee and motions* NIGEL *to sit beside her on* L. *of settee. Meanwhile,* HILDA *sits in chair* R.)

MRS. HADFIELD. Thank you— Well, now, I hear our two children have had a little contretemps together— (*Almost gaily.*) Well, young married people do have their little contretemps from time to time. What do you say, Avril?

AVRIL. Look, Mrs. Hadfield—

> (*Masking her from* MRS. HADFIELD, FRED *puts his hand over her mouth and stops her speaking.*)

MRS. HADFIELD. Well, Avril?

FRED (*with his hand still over* AVRIL's *mouth*). I'm afraid our Avril's too full for words at the moment.

HILDA. Yes, the poor girl's been bowled over by the shock.

FRED (*removing his hand from her mouth and tapping* AVRIL's *shoulder to make his points*). It's been most distressing—most! She couldn't bring herself to tell us. We had to drag the facts out of her.

HILDA (*very dignified*). We're not used to kitchen-sink behaviour— not in our family.

FRED (*very dignified*). Now, Mother, it's not in order for us to say things like that— It's up to us to set the tone and view it as dignified as possible—circumstances being what they are.

MRS. HADFIELD. I think the matter can easily be settled by leaving the young people alone together.

FRED. I'm sorry, Mrs. Hadfield, but I don't think we could persuade our Avril to be left alone with your Nigel—not after this morning's revelations.

MRS. HADFIELD. But Nigel has something to say to her.

FRED. Well, he can say it here, can't he?

> (*Pause.*)

MRS. HADFIELD. You'd better say it, Nigel.

NIGEL. What, here, Mother?

MRS. HADFIELD. Yes, Nigel—here.

NIGEL. Now, Mother?

MRS. HADFIELD. Yes, now.

NIGEL. Very well. (*He rises, clears his throat and recites with a self-conscious, high-pitched voice.*) Avril, my wife! I have behaved as a most corrupt, depraved and degenerate beast. I do not deny that after the cup-tie, for one deeply regrettable and most humiliating moment, I allowed my blood to run riot and my flesh to take the wrong turning. However, I swear to you, Avril, I shall remember the incident for the rest of my life.

MRS. HADFIELD (*prompting hastily*). —with shame.

NIGEL. Yes, Mother. With shame.

MRS. HADFIELD. Go on, then, Nigel.

NIGEL. I—er—

MRS. HADFIELD. Speak up!

NIGEL (*even higher pitched*). It was an experience that I—er—er— (*He is stuck.*) Well—er— (*With a spurt of confidence.*) Taking it by and large, I assure you it was a lesson!

MRS. HADFIELD. Say you're sorry.

NIGEL. What?

MRS. HADFIELD. You're sorry!

NIGEL. Oh, yes— I'm truly sorry, Avril. I'm utterly repentant and if only you'll come back to me I think you'll find after this I shall forever be at your service. (*Pause.*) What do you say, Avril? (*He sits.*)

MRS. HADFIELD. Yes, what do you say, Avril?

HILDA. Say what's in your mind, Avril.

FRED. Well, Avril, what have you decided to say?

AVRIL. I want to divorce him.

MRS. HADFIELD (*rises*). Divorce him!

AVRIL. Yes, Mrs. Hadfield—for misconducting.

MRS. HADFIELD. Miscon—? But you can't!

AVRIL. Why not?

MRS. HADFIELD (*frightened*). But you can't—you simply can't—not divorce. Not in these circumstances. (*Moving slightly to* R. *of* HILDA.) I mean, if his affections had been regularly taken elsewhere *perhaps* —but one single evening with a member of the frail sisterhood—

NIGEL. Mother, it was only twenty minutes and she was a—

MRS. HADFIELD (*turning on him*). Do be quiet, Nigel! Avril, if you really feel you can't forgive, then I suggest the only proper course is for us to arrange a nice, quiet case of desertion.

AVRIL. But you have to wait for a desertion, don't you?

MRS. HADFIELD. It's only a matter of three short years.

AVRIL. Three short years! (*She moves across stage to her mother,* R. *and kneels. Alarmed.*) Mother, I can't do that. I might have lost my bloom by then.

HILDA (*comforting her*). It can't be expected of you, love. It can't be expected of you.

MRS. HADFIELD. I do hope, Mrs. Midway, you realize the implications if she refuses.

HILDA. What implications, Mrs. Hadfield?

MRS. HADFIELD. What implications? I'm sure you've considered them, Mr. Midway.

FRED. I've weighed them up, yes.

MRS. HADFIELD. Then you realise there'll be some nasty aspersions cast at your daughter even if she is the innocent party.

FRED (*feigned innocence, moving* U.S. *behind settee and then* D.R. *to between* MRS. HADFIELD *and* HILDA's *chair*). Aspersions? I don't think there'll be any aspersions.

MRS. HADFIELD (*controlled anger*). Well, I assure you she won't get away with it lightly, not if she's going to play this kind of game. I'll see to that.

FRED. Now then, Mrs. Hadfield, there's no need to be vindictive.

MRS. HADFIELD (*angry*). I expect she's out to drain our family of every penny. You don't think I'm stupid, do you? I can guess who put her up to it.

(NIGEL *rises and moves* U.L. *to french windows*.)

FRED. And what do you mean by that?

MRS. HADFIELD (*threateningly*). You know what I mean!

FRED (*feigned amazement and fury*). Wait a minute—wait a minute! I can't get over it! Here's my daughter, the picture of radiant innocence deceived by your son, that gay Lothario over there—and now all you can do is add insinuations and threats on top.

MRS. HADFIELD. And they're threats I'll carry out. You needn't worry about that. Let me remind you that we have a certain amount of influence in our family.

AVRIL (*bursts out*). Not now his uncle's cut him off!

(*Pause. Everyone stares at* AVRIL. FRED, *exasperated with her, turns and pushes his fingers through his hair with a "game's up" gesture.*)

MRS. HADFIELD (*moving to* NIGEL U.L.). Did you tell her your uncle had cut you off?

NIGEL. Well, Mother, I did mention it.

(*If looks could kill,* NIGEL *would be dead by now. Pause.*)

MRS. HADFIELD (*slowly dawns on her*). Oh? (*She moves forward* D.S.L.) Oh-oh? (*She stops still.*) Oh!

NIGEL. What's wrong, then?

MRS. HADFIELD. What's wrong? We know now! We understand it all now! So the Midway family is up to its tricks again, is it?

FRED. If you take my advice, Mrs. Hadfield, you'll count ten—slowly, like. Slander can be a very grave issue and there are witnesses.

MRS. HADFIELD. There's no slander in what I'm going to say— This family, this rag-tag and bob-tail family of nobodies, appears from nowhere—and worms its way into the very cream of Dowlihull society! And how? By taking advantage of the kindness, integrity and high-mindedness of my son, Nigel. Isn't that so, Nigel?

NIGEL. Definitely—most definitely.

HILDA (*rises and moves to* C.). Now look here, Mrs. Hadfield—

MRS. HADFIELD (*shouting her down*). How did she get to marry him in the first place? I'll tell you how. She robbed my Nigel of his innocence—put him in a compromising position—and then threatened to sue him for breach of promise.

FRED. Have you quite finished, Mrs. Hadfield?

MRS. HADFIELD. No, I have not quite finished. Having used every means to exploit the Hadfield family, you now learn that my son might not have the financial expectations you'd been hoping for. That's what this stupid divorce is about, nothing more nor less.

FRED (*sarcastically*). So that's all it's about, is it? Well, you might change your mind when you read the headlines: "Young Husband Spends Night in Soho Brothel".

MRS. HADFIELD. Very well. You are forcing me to reveal something it would be best to keep secret.

FRED. Now don't try to bluff me, Mrs. Hadfield.

MRS. HADFIELD. I promised my dear husband I'd only mention it in an emergency.

FRED. Mention what?

MRS. HADFIELD. I think it would be best to discuss it in front of as few people as possible. Nigel, go to the car—and stay there!

NIGEL. Certainly, Mother.

MRS. HADFIELD. I shall join you in a moment.

(NIGEL *leaves through hall door.*)

FRED. Here, what is all this?

MRS. HADFIELD. If you wish to hear what I have to say, I think your daughter had better retire, too.

(*Pause.*)

FRED (*with immense dignity*). Mother, take Avril to our kitchen-dinette.

HILDA (*rises*). Avril!

(AVRIL *and* HILDA *walk haughtily with their noses in the air past* MRS. HADFIELD *and out through the kitchen door.*)

FRED. Well?

MRS. HADFIELD (*crosses to* D.L.). My dear husband has recently encountered certain information while examining the return forms at the Inland Revenue.

FRED. There's nothing wrong with my Income Tax. He can say what he likes; I've got the best accountant in the district.

MRS. HADFIELD. Your return form isn't in question, Mr. Midway. No, it's a statement on someone else's—someone very close to you.

FRED (*moving* L. *to* MRS. HADFIELD). Someone close to me? Now what are you getting at? What is this? Blackmail? (*Moving to* D.R.) You tell your dear husband from me that whatever he's discovered on Income Tax forms he'd better keep his mouth shut about it—or your dear husband will soon be down the Social Security.

MRS. HADFIELD (*moving to* R. *of settee. Almost sweetly*). You needn't be worried on his behalf, Mr. Midway. I think he'd soon get another appointment elsewhere. (*Sugary.*) You see, people will be very sympathetic when he tells them he only revealed certain personal matters to save your family from a case of bigamy.

FRED. Huh?

MRS. HADFIELD. I wonder if you'd care to ask your Eileen's boy-friend —Robert, isn't it—how his wife's getting on.

FRED (*stunned*). Wife?

MRS. HADFIELD. I expect Eileen knows about his little difficulties— After all, she's just spent a week at the sea-side with him, hasn't she? Oh, yes, he's got a wife—he makes her a very generous allowance, too, according to his Income Tax form— Of course, if you persist in your stupid attack upon my son, I'm afraid it will be our painful duty to inform Robert's wife of his adultery and indicate that your daughter Eileen is the co-respondent— Well, I only hope all this hasn't made us late for church. (*She walks to the door.*) Nigel and I will be returning after the service to collect Avril—so you've got a little over an hour to make her see reason.

FRED (*lost. Stumbling to* C.). Just a minute, Mrs. Hadfield.

MRS. HADFIELD (*moving* D.S. *a little*). Yes, what is it? We shall make Avril's apologies to the Vicar, naturally—Well?

FRED (*dazed and then with a slight sarcastic smile*). I only hope—it's a nice—sermon.

MRS. HADFIELD (*coldly*). Thank you. Don't worry. We shall be back. (*She leaves by hall door.*)

FRED (*turning* U.S., *floundering and calling out as a child in trouble*). Mo-o-om!

CURTAIN

ACT TWO

As the curtain rises, FRED *repeats his action of moving* U.S., *calling:*

FRED. Mo-o-om!

(HILDA *opens the kitchen door.*)

HILDA. What is it, love?

FRED. Come in here.

HILDA. She's gone?

(FRED *nods in a dazed manner.* HILDA *is now* U.C. FRED *is to her* L.)

(*Alarmed.*) Fred! What has that woman said to you?

FRED (*shattered*). Something terrible. If it's true—it's something appalling.

HILDA. Tell me, love—tell me.

FRED. She says that Bob—

HILDA. Yes, dear?

FRED. She says he's a married man!

HILDA. Married—man?

(FRED *nods his head miserably and wanders to his chair* D.L.)

Married man—Bob?

FRED (*sitting*). He must be— He's declared it on his Income Tax.

HILDA (*moving down* L., *trembling*). O-o-o-ooo. O-o-o-ooo. O-o-o-ooo.

FRED. I feel the same way myself.

HILDA (*aghast*). But our Eileen's just spent a week's holiday with him — Married man! He can't be!

FRED. It's on his Income Tax, Mother. You have to show your lines for that—otherwise everybody would be claiming.

(HILDA *marches* U.S. *to the inter-com phone. She picks up the receiver.*)

What are you doing?

HILDA. Send for him! Send for him and ask him to his face!

FRED. All in good time, love, all in good time. We've got to make our calculations first.

HILDA. Calculations?

FRED. We never rush into anything till we've calculated our position. That's the rule, Mother.

HILDA. But, Fred—

FRED. No buts, love. If we can only keep our heads, we don't know what might accrue.

HILDA. He's a married man!

FRED (rises). All right, he's a married man—but let's have nothing spontaneous, if you don't mind.

(HILDA puts the phone down. She shakes her head emotionally.)

HILDA (moving L. towards FRED). What are we going to do?

FRED (moving to D.R.). I don't know yet, love. We've got to think about it.

HILDA (now at L. of settee). It fits in now. It all fits in.

FRED. What does?

HILDA. Spending a whole week with him—and not even getting her engagement ring. I knew one of ours couldn't be that slow.

FRED (moving to U.R. of settee). It comes back to me now.

HILDA. What does?

FRED (moving to D.R.C.). I think Bob was trying to enlighten me as to the position earlier this morning—only I was too busy with my locos to listen.

HILDA (moving in front of settee L.). You think Eileen knows he's a married man, then?

FRED. She must do.

HILDA (shocked. Towards audience). That's dreadful! Our own daughter having dealings like that!

FRED. What's worse, Mother—there's no future in it. (Perplexed. To audience.) To think that a daughter of mine could be wasting her sexual efforts!

HILDA (sitting on settee. Slowly and thoughtfully). So that woman's blackmailing us, is she?

FRED (lost in thought). What?

HILDA. Mrs. Hadfield's blackmailing us?

FRED. That's it.

HILDA. If we expose her Nigel, she'll expose our Eileen?

FRED. In public.

HILDA (rising rapidly and moving U.L. to the inter-com phone). Well, don't just stand there, Dad—bring Bob and Eileen up here. Find out the whole truth behind it.

FRED (moving U.R. a little). Patience, Mother, will you! I'm trying to work something out.

HILDA. We'll have to hand back our Avril. That's the only way we can settle it—and hand back our Avril before things go too far.

FRED (sitting on R. end of settee). Mother! If you don't mind—

HILDA (*now behind him to his* L. *Sudden idea*). Here! Why not order
Bob never to see our Eileen again?

FRED. What?

HILDA (*moving round* L. *of settee*). They've been on holiday together,
but nobody can prove whether they have or they haven't. Order
Bob to sever his connections.

FRED. I can't do that.

HILDA (*sitting on* L. *end of settee*). Why not?

FRED. I've got too much of his firm's equipment down in my workshop there. If he leaves, he'll have to put it back in the store— And
that'll mean the end of my locos— And if I lose my locos, I shall be
losing my intros— (*Making a pedalling movement with one foot.*)
That'll mean back on my bike—collectin' door to door.

HILDA (*alarmed*). You couldn't do that again—not collecting door to
door. It'd be so lowering. I mean, the whole neighbourhood would
be talking about it.

FRED (*pathetically and tragically*). What else is there, then? All my
chances of high-class intros taken away from me— No more friendly
chats-ups in the board room. No more signing contracts over
lunch. If we hand over our Avril, the Hadfields will still be turned
against us—the uncle will still have Nigel cut off— But to risk losing
my locos—never! How could I appear up the club track on a Sunday
afternoon—mixing with all the nobs of Dowlihull—chatting like a
brother about the size of my flue and my water capacity—when I
haven't even got a workshop to back me up!

HILDA. We'll have to sacrifice our Avril, then—order her back?

FRED (*very sad*). Poor little Avril.

HILDA. Poor little Avril. Fancy our Eileen bringing this upon us.
How could she! Knowingly carry on with a married man?

FRED. Yes, how could she? "Knowingly." (*He queries this.*) "Knowingly?" (*A thought strikes him. He rises. He beams and with delight
spreads out the word.*) Know-ing-lee?

HILDA (*surprised*). What's the matter?

FRED. She mustn't know.

HILDA. Mustn't know? But she does know! We've just proved she
knows.

FRED (*moving* D.L.). Quiet, Mother! Quiet! (*He claps his hand to his
brow and thinks.*) It's coming— Yes, it's slowly coming. Wait a
minute! Wait a minute! Yes, it's it! I've got it!

HILDA. Got what?

FRED. Eileen mustn't know—she must act innocent. She must swear
that she thought he was single.

HILDA. She must what?

FRED. Listen to this, love! Listen to this! Bob's wife divorces him. (*Pause.*) Our Eileen is named as co-respondent—

HILDA (*howls*). Oh!

FRED. Shut up blarting— I haven't finished. Bob then asks Eileen for her hand in marriage—

HILDA. And about time, too.

FRED. —but she refuses.

HILDA (*amazed*). Refuses?

FRED. Yes. Refuses! (*Slowly. Pointed.*) Because she never knew he was a married man. (*With exaggerated histrionics thrown out towards the audience.*) He begs her—but she is adamant— She openly declares, "He might have taken my virtue, but he'll never take my soul!" How's that for a public front, eh? We'll be the most virtuous family for miles around. What a picture for the district—what a picture! Innocence betrayed! Perfect. Why, a man might even insure a cathedral out of that! (*He moves* U.L.)

HILDA. But you're forgetting something— What about Bob?

FRED. What about him?

HILDA. If Mrs. Hadfield starts spreading the dirt around, how can we have him in the house?

FRED (*moving to* U.R.). Oh, it should take a week or two for us to realize publicly what a scoundrel the man is. In the meantime, I'll get all the know-how I can out of him. After that, it's a pure gentleman's agreement between us.

HILDA. How do you mean?

FRED (*now at* R. *end of settee*). In exchange for the equipment which he whips from his firm, we'll allow him to have the occasional discreet carry-on with our daughter. Goodwill on both sides! Tacit understanding! I doubt whether we'll even have to mention it.

HILDA. But they mustn't be seen together in public.

FRED (*moving* D.R. *to audience*). Of course not! Fortunately, they haven't got the first carefree seething rage of youth upon 'em, have they? No, I think a long weekend together once a month—plus the odd bit of car work at night up Snoggers'-Alley-Back-of-the-Airport ought to keep 'em simmered down nicely— (*Moving to* HILDA *and sitting on* R. *end of settee.*) It'll all turn out so beautifully respectable, I assure you. We're in, Benjamin—we're in!

(AVRIL *enters from kitchen and remains* U.L.)

AVRIL. What's all the noise about, Dad?

FRED (*excitedly*). Avril, my love, virtue is always triumphant as long as enough people know about it. Never forget that.

AVRIL (*moving to* L. *of settee*). What's he on about, Mom?

HILDA (*almost weeping with joy*). Any emergency and you can rely upon him. He's a wonderful man. Your father's a marvellous man!

AVRIL. Does that mean I can get rid of Nigel?

FRED (*jumping up excitedly*). It's better than I thought—better than I thought! (*Moving* D.R.) Bob forgot he was married, so did Nigel— My two incorruptible, stainless daughters, one the mistress, the other the wife—defend their honour against male inconstancy! With such a sterling, pure, noble family to back up his insurance policies, how could a man go wrong? (*He casts his eyes upwards and exclaims.*) Lord! Can you hear me? I don't deserve it! (*Explaining his action.*) Well, Mrs. Hadfield's in touch. Why shouldn't I be?

AVRIL. Is he all right, Mother?

HILDA (*rising and moving to* FRED D.R. *Still in her ecstasy*). A wonderful man—a simply marvellous man!

FRED (*moving rapidly to* AVRIL *and ushering her out*). You'd better get back in our kitchen-dinette, Avril. There's a lot of water got to run under sewers-or-wherever-it-is before we've finished. (*He closes the kitchen door on her and moves to the inter-com phone* U.C.) Now then, Mother, I think we'd better investigate friend Robert's nuptial disorders, don't you? We want the facts straight, don't we? And it's only right and proper I should do a bit of the irate father. It's expected. (*He picks up the phone and turns the handle. During this conversation* HILDA *sits on the settee*.). Bob? How are you doing down there, old man?— You've found the leak, have you? What? Eileen did?— Splendid— Just below the union pipe? Who'd have thought it?— No. Bob, as a matter of fact, I'd like you to come up here for a little private discussion— I'm afraid it's something that's been reported to me in your connection and needs immediate clarification— No, no, no, it's nothing for you to worry about— not really—I think— What? You'll come up straight away? Wonderful! Well, see you, then. (*He puts down the phone.*)

HILDA. I must say you didn't sound very irate. Aren't you going to put your indignation on with him a bit?

FRED (*moving* R. *of settee*). Mother, you don't understand. Those words were business expressions specifically calculated to put the wind up anybody— Besides, the best hold you've got over your neighbour is to keep him guessing—wondering where the chop's coming from.

HILDA. I see.

FRED (*sincerely*). My dear, it's in the civilized order of things. One man must be able to drop another in the cart when he wants—how else could we have united effort?

(*During the following speeches there must be a touch of wistfulness, a sad recognition of themselves.*)

HILDA. You've got a manner, Father, there's no doubt. Sometimes I think it's wonderful—rising as we have—the way we've learnt gentility. I expect they're proud of you—the Sunlight Assurance must be very proud of you.

FRED. Proud? That's a strange word— No, love, a man's alone in the Sunlight. Talent counts for something, I suppose—having the right intros counts for a good deal more. (*He joins* HILDA *on the settee, sitting to her* R.) Some people are born with the right intros. If I ever had grandchildren, I'd like 'em to be born with that.

HILDA. I know you would, dear. You're a great family man. It's the family that's always uppermost with you.

FRED. If only I could have a grandchild who actually went to a public school.

HILDA. Is that your ambition, dear?

FRED. There are one or two real public-school men up at the track, you know. Not like what I pretend to be sometimes—but real. When I speak to them I know my correspondence courses can only ever take me so far— Those chaps, somehow, seem to have their education ingrained.

HILDA (*reassuring him*). You're every bit as good as them, Father—you've got the classy cut and the talk to go with it.

FRED (*sighs*). No—no, I haven't.

HILDA. Oh yes, you have.

FRED. I haven't.

HILDA. You have. Of course you have.

FRED (*smiles tenderly*). What would I do without you?

(FRED *and* HILDA *embrace. At the same time* BOB *and* EILEEN *enter with their hands joined. They see* FRED *and* HILDA *kissing, so they, too, give each other a kiss.* FRED *parts from his embrace, sees* EILEEN *and* BOB *kissing, jumps to his feet and marches up to* BOB *and taps him on the shoulder.*)

(U.L.) Now, now, that's enough of that. Mother! Take Eileen into the kitchen-dinette, will you? Only don't talk about things—not in front of Avril there.

HILDA (*moving round the settee* R. *and towards the kitchen*). Come along Eileen.

EILEEN. What is all this?

HILDA. They've got some serious man-to-manning to get through.

FRED. Eileen, would you mind leaving us? You'll be fully informed of the situation in due course, I've no doubt.

HILDA (*opening the kitchen door and ordering her in*). Eileen!

    (HILDA *and* EILEEN *enter the kitchen.*)

FRED. Do sit down, Bob.

    (FRED *gestures* BOB *to sit in the chair* D.R. BOB *does so and* FRED *stands to his* L., *studying him. Pause.*)

BOB. Well?

FRED (*almost as if dictating a letter. Very formal voice*). I hope you will not be offended by what I am about to moot— I am not denying that untoward misinformation might have arisen in your case and laid at my feet—but I think the weight of evidence that we have in hand points pretty conclusively in a single and deeply regrettable direction. You will therefore note that I am very much placing the matter on an official footing—by which I mean, however cordial our relationship might have been in the past, the time has now arrived for a simple, straightforward and authoritative answer to a formal question I am about to put to you. I think the tone in which I am expressing myself might indicate as much.

BOB. What is it, Mr. Midway?

FRED. To speak bluntly: have you heretofore made any prior contractual arrangements with a member of the opposite sex?

BOB. You mean—am I married?

FRED. I think that nicely sums it up.

BOB. Who told you?

FRED. Never mind who told me. Are you or aren't you?

BOB. I am.

FRED. You are?

BOB. Yes.

FRED. Are you sure?

BOB. I said so.

FRED. Wait a minute. Wait a minute. (*He moves to the kitchen door and opens it.*) Mother!

HILDA (*appearing. Whispers*). Yes?

FRED (*whispers*). He is.

HILDA (*whispers*). He is?

FRED (*nods*). He is.

HILDA (*glaring at* BOB). I thought as much.

FRED. I'll keep you informed.

HILDA. You do. (*She leaves.*)

    (FRED *closes the door and moves to* L. *end of settee.*)

FRED. Well now! We've established it, haven't we? And why haven't we been told of this?

BOB. I didn't think it was necessary.

FRED. Not necessary?

BOB. You might not have understood. I mean—it is a very respectable family.

FRED. I'm glad you recognize it as such.

BOB. If you'd found out, you might have put up some barrier between Eileen and me—it's as simple as that.

FRED. Simple as that? Simple as that! Have you read your marriage policy? You've contracted with some woman a life warranty without options. You look it through, my lad—it's in the Prayer Book. I know, 'cos I went through it most carefully before I was married—and you won't find any space for endorsements.

BOB. What if she abrogates the agreement—what then?

FRED. Abrogates the agreement?

BOB. I consider the covenant between us no longer obtains, as she's arbitrarily rescinded one of the major clauses.

FRED. Your wife has? (*He draws up the pouffe to* L. *of* BOB's *chair and sits on it. They talk confidentially.*) What's she done, then? Gone off with a fancy man?

(BOB *shakes his head.*)

BOB. To put the facts before you: I was offered this managership at the local branch of the Light Craft Engineering Company—and she wouldn't come with me.

FRED. Wouldn't come with you?

BOB. She said she wouldn't leave London to come and live in Dowlihull.

FRED (*amazed*). She'd rather live in London than Dowlihull! But this is the nicest residential district in the whole length and breadth.

BOB. What could I do but leave her down there? After all, a man has to look after his career, doesn't he?

FRED. Quite right, lad! Quite right! A most sensible attitude.

BOB. I've been up here eighteen months and as far as I'm concerned, she's deserted me. I've looked through that Church service pretty thoroughly and she's the one who's broken the contract. There's a clause in it that says she's got to stay by me and she hasn't.

FRED. There is? You don't mind if we check up, do you? (*He goes to the kitchen door.*) Mother!

HILDA (*appearing*). Yes, dear?

FRED. Fetch me the Prayer Book.

HILDA. Prayer Book? What Prayer Book?

FRED (*impatiently*). The ivory-coloured thing what you carried up the aisle.

HILDA. What do you want that for?

FRED. Don't ask. Just get it.

HILDA (*thinks. Then*). Oh, I know where it is! It's in my souvenir drawer! (*She removes it from the sideboard* U.L. *and gives it to him.*)

FRED. Thanks.

HILDA. Is that all?

FRED. That's all.

(HILDA *re-enters the kitchen.*)

Right, then! Let's get a few stonewall facts behind us. (*Giving* BOB *the Prayer Book.*) Where's her infringement—show me! (*Encouraging* BOB *as he searches in the Prayer Book.*) Go on, Bob, find me a *sine qua non* in that lot!

(BOB *rises and looking through the Frayer Book moves to* C. *Meanwhile* FRED *has moved to* D.L.)

BOB. Here you are!

FRED (*moves to* BOB). Where?

BOB. There. "Forsaking all others, keep thee only unto him."

FRED (*Takes the Prayer Book and studying it moves farther* D.L.). Let's have a look— Yes, you're quite right. It's here in black and white. (*Counting.*) Paragraph one, two, three, four, five—clause two—item two. And what's more, she says, "I will" straight after. (*To* BOB.) I suppose she did say, "I will"?

BOB. Loud and clear.

FRED. Well, you've got her there then, haven't you? She can't wriggle out of that one. (*Moving to* BOB.) You know, you ought to be in insurance— As soon as I saw you, I said to myself, "There's a chap who knows where he's going. There's a chap who wouldn't commit himself, not without reading the lines in detail." (*Glancing at the book.*) I suppose the law of the land will uphold you? (*To audience.*) 'cos what's legal isn't always moral—as we are undoubtedly aware.

BOB. Oh, yes, I've looked up the legal aspects and there's no doubt about it, she's deserted me.

(*They are both* D.S.C. *looking towards the audience.* FRED *puts his arm round* BOB'S *shoulders.*)

FRED (*sentimentally*). Splendid, Bob, splendid. I'm proud of you—d'you know that? I'm proud of you.

BOB (*sentimentally*). Well, I haven't been working with you on the locos all these months, not to be influenced by the power of your shrewdness and thought, Mr. Midway.

FRED (*sentimentally*). Yes, there'll be status coming out of them locos—and that'll mean good money for the pair of us.

Bob (*sentimentally*). It's surprising what can happen when you get to know a few of the right people.

Fred. You've got the right sentiments, Bob. We're going to set each other up. (*Pause.*) My own children are all passion and emotion. D'you know, you're nearer to me than anybody: clear, level-headed, discerning. Somehow, I feel as though you're my son.

Bob. Perhaps soon—I'll be your son-in-law.

Fred (*penny dropping*). Son-in-law? . . . Eileen? . . . Eileen! (*Alarmed, he breaks from* Bob *and moves* D.L.) Wait a minute, wait a minute! (*Returning to* Bob.) What's all this about divorcing your wife for desertion? (*Emphatic.*) She's got you for illicit goings-on with my eldest daughter!

(*During the following* Bob *backs away from* Fred *while* Fred *is constantly moving towards him. This movement is continued round the stage in a clockwise direction. As* Fred *passes the table, he slams down the Prayer Book on it.*)

Bob. But Mr. Midway—

Fred (*cutting in*). All this about legality and contracts and policies— you've been leading me up the garden path! You've been blinding me with science! What's more, it's my own blinding science!

Bob. But, Mr. Midway—

Fred. Treating me like one of my own clients—bolstering up my ego—chatting on about what comes closest to my heart: money, respectability and my civic pride in Dowlihull! Learnt from me? I reckon you've learnt a bit too much!

Bob. But, Mr. Midway—

Fred. You listen to me—no buts. Have you or have you not been carrying on with our Eileen?

(*They have now returned to* C. *stage.* Bob *is on* Fred's R.)

Bob. Look, Mr. Midway, I assure you, as soon as I have my freedom I'll marry her.

Fred. And drag her with you through the divorce courts first—is that the idea?

Bob. Of course not— We've been most discreet in every way.

Fred. Oh, have you? Well, how did I know you were a married man?

Bob. What?

Fred. How did I know you were already married?

Bob. I assume because Eileen's told her mother—and her mother's told you.

Fred. Well, she hasn't. I've heard about it from a third party.

Bob. A third party?

FRED. Yes, a third party. (*Shaking his head gravely.*) And as an insurance man, I can tell you that means big trouble straight off. (*He walks away from him to* U.S.C. *More relaxed.*) So Eileen knows you're a married man, does she?

BOB (*crossing to* L. *and sitting in the chair*). I thought it best to be frank and honest.

FRED (*tense again*). Frank and honest! I'd have thought you'd have had a bit more decency about you than to be frank and honest! You've made her a party to your misdemeanour—that's what you've done. All frank and honest means is: "Here's my guilt; now you carry it for a bit."

BOB. I'm sorry.

FRED (*moves to the kitchen door*). I don't know what kind of a family you come from, but just remember—we've got standards in this. (*He opens the kitchen door.*) Mother!

HILDA (*entering*). Yes, dear?

FRED. It's true. She knows.

HILDA. She knows?

FRED. I'm just letting you know she knows.

HILDA. Did he tell her?

FRED. He's young, Mother. He hasn't got our experience.

HILDA. Silly boy! Silly, silly boy!

FRED (*moving to* L. *of* BOB's *chair*). Forget you ever told her, lad, and everything will be all right.

BOB. Is that all, then?

FRED. All? Well, what else is there?

BOB. Aren't you going to throw me out of the house or anything?

FRED. Throw you out of the house! (*Smiles and moves to* C.) Well, there's no doubt you've committed a variety of indiscretions, but I think we can have a gentleman's agreement over the whole business should eventualities arise. For the moment, I should like you to do just one thing.

BOB (*rising*). What's that?

FRED. Get back down the shed and finish repairing the union pipe.

HILDA. You'll still be going up the track, then, this afternoon?

FRED. What? I've got to go up the track whatever happens. If we don't have my King George the Fifth doing half a dozen circuits, there'll be a lot of talk among the club members, I can tell you. (*To* BOB.) "Letting down the side"—"Can't afford to run them" . . . That's the way you get your bad name.

BOB (*moving to French windows*). I'd better get down there, then.

FRED. You'd better, lad—you'd better.

(BOB *leaves.* FRED *follows him to the french window and calls:*)
I'll be with you in half a tick! (FRED *hurries back to* HILDA, *who has moved to* C., *and says confidentially:*) That lad's married with a wife in London who refuses to live in Dowlihull.

HILDA (*amazed*). Refuses to live in Dowlihull?

FRED. I was staggered an' all— As soon as he's free, he wants to marry our Eileen.

HILDA. He does?

FRED. Yes. So, taking it all in all, I find his circumstances very mitigating—very mitigating indeed.

HILDA. And he has worked himself up to be manager—and he speaks well.

FRED. Exactly.

HILDA. On top of which—although please don't breathe it to her face—I think our Eileen's sands are running out a little bit, don't you?

FRED. Yes. That's a point to be considered.

HILDA. So what do we do?

FRED. What do we do? Exactly what we planned: she's not to know he's a married man—so if the case does come up, she's got enraged innocence on her side. Excuse me—the union pipe. (*He moves to the french windows.*)

HILDA. But what happens after?

FRED. After?

HILDA. Does she marry him or not?

FRED (*he returns*). All things being equal, it'd be better if she didn't— But seeing as how her sands are running out or as the poet once put it, "Time's wingèd chariot is giving her a nudge"—I think we might allow her to forgive him and marry him in four or five years' time very discreetly—and certainly in another area altogether. Right, then, Mother, it's all up to you— Get on with it. (*He moves to the french windows.* HILDA *follows him.*)

HILDA. Eh?

FRED. A kind, gentle, understanding chat between mother and daughter—woman's work! A union pipe is a man's! (*He moves off rapidly through the french windows.*)
(HILDA *draws herself together, thinking with joy of the responsibility which* FRED *has just allotted her. She opens the kitchen door.*)

HILDA. Eileen dear—just a little wordy, if you don't mind.
(AVRIL *comes out before* EILEEN.)

AVRIL. What's been settled about me and Nigel?

HILDA. All in good time, Avril, all in good time. I'd just like a little wordy with Eileen first.

(*They are all* U.S. AVRIL R., EILEEN C., HILDA L.)

AVRIL. I'm the one the fuss is supposed to be about. Nobody'd think it the way I've been stuck in that kitchen.

HILDA. You've had Eileen to talk to.

AVRIL. Oh yes, a fine lot of sympathy I get out of Eileen.

EILEEN. I listened, didn't I?

AVRIL. Yes, with a glassy stare. (*Moving* D.S.) Mind you, it's what I expect. After all, I not only managed to marry a man, but I've now decided to chuck him up.

EILEEN (*following her. Furious*). And what exactly do you mean by that?

HILDA. Avril! Do you mind going back in the kitchen-dinette?

EILEEN. You leave her, Mother! I want to know what she means.

AVRIL (*now* D.C.). She's been jealous of me ever since I was in the cradle, hasn't she, Mom?

EILEEN (*now* D.L.C.). All right, then, Avril—you've got your man, and very cunning you were to get him—but now he's turned out to be as stupid as you are, you ought to stick by him.

AVRIL. Did you hear what she said, Mother? Did you hear that? And me the injured party!

HILDA (*moving in between them*). Now, Eileen, whatever your feelings, hold your tongue. Please!

AVRIL. Are you siding with her?

HILDA. No!

AVRIL. If you're siding with her, that's the last straw, that is.

HILDA. I just don't want any silly squabbles and that's enough! Now then, Avril, get back in the kitchen-dinette!

AVRIL (*moving* U.L. *slightly*). I know perfectly well what you're going to talk about, so I don't see why I shouldn't stay.

HILDA. You don't.

AVRIL. Oh yes, I do. Dad let the cat out of the bag when he was going on all exotic a bit ago.

HILDA. He what?

AVRIL (*to* EILEEN). Your Bob's a married man, isn't he? (*Pause.*) I thought you'd have to end up scraping somebody else's barrel.

EILEEN. Let me get hold of her! Just let me get hold of her!

(HILDA *holds back* EILEEN.)

HILDA. Eileen! (*Sharply.*) Avril! Into the kitchen-dinette. Now go on, quick!

AVRIL (*at the door*). If you're all that short, I'm putting Nigel back on the market soon—but I doubt whether he'd look at you! (*She leaves.*)

HILDA. She doesn't know what she's saying, Eileen. The poor girl's distraught. It's all been such a blow to her.

EILEEN (*moving* U.R. *slightly*). How did Dad know Bob's a married man?

HILDA (*sitting on* R. *end of settee*). We're not too upset about it, Eileen, so don't worry. You'll find your parents can be most understanding.

EILEEN (*insistent*). How did he find out?

HILDA. Well, as a matter of fact, Mrs. Hadfield told him.

EILEEN. She knew?

HILDA. She got it from her husband—he saw it on some Income Tax forms.

EILEEN. I see.

HILDA. Now come and sit down, Eileen—do sit down. 'cos I'd like to talk it all over with you nice-and-motherly-like—if that suits.

(EILEEN *sits on* L. *end of settee*.)

That's right, love. That's right. Me and your father have been over all the pros and cons. And we must say we're very sympathetic towards your difficulties—we just don't know why you haven't confided in us before.

EILEEN. Mother, I haven't told you because I thought you wouldn't approve. (*With head aloft*.) You see, my relationship with Bob has been an honest, forthright acceptance of our physical needs. I'm not ashamed of having a sex-life—in fact, I'm proud of it. But it's not what you might call the respectable way of going on, is it?

HILDA (*reassuringly*). Eileen, it's only by a chance coincidence that anybody's found out—so I should say you've been most respectable over the matter myself— Besides, we're not what you might call narrow-minded and you do happen to be thirty next birthday.

EILEEN (*hurt*). What's that got to do with it?

HILDA. Circumstances being what they are for you, we expected you to show some human behaviour eventually. Your father and I have no objection to a certain degree of human behaviour—as long as it doesn't appear beyond the four walls.

EILEEN. But it has, hasn't it?

HILDA. Well, yes, it has—and that's what we're frightened of. That's why, whatever rumours might be flying round, you must never admit you know he's a married man.

EILEEN. I must what?

HILDA. If Bob's wife got to know, you might be cited as the scarlet woman in the case.

EILEEN. Well, I am, aren't I?

HILDA. Yes, but you must never admit to it! We'd have to leave the

district if you did that— No, you must say he always claimed he
was single—and he happened to seduce you strictly on those terms.
Now, after the Court's found him guilty—

EILEEN. Guilty of what?

HILDA. Misconduct, of course—he'll ask you to marry him. That's
when you refuse.

EILEEN. I what?

HILDA. You refuse— You say out loud he's abused your innocence
and if you'd known he was married you wouldn't have let him
touch you with a barge-pole.

EILEEN. And why exactly do I do that?

HILDA. For the neighbours—who do you think? You'll have a lot
of sympathy. (*Imagining it.*) For a little indiscretion—you go a
spinster to the grave.

EILEEN. But, Mother—!

HILDA (*rising and moving* D.S. *To audience, romantically*). One moment
of weakness and a lifetime of sorrow—I can hear the hushed voices
as they breathe your name.

EILEEN. Mother, what on earth are you talking about?

HILDA (*to* EILEEN). You'll be able to slip away for week-ends with
him—after a few years settle elsewhere and get married. (*To
audience.*) But for the neighbours, you'll always be a rose—a white
rose, perhaps nibbled slightly by a caterpillar—but still a white rose!

EILEEN (*rising and moving* D.S. *to* L. *of* HILDA). Very touching, I must
say—but aren't you getting things a bit distorted?

HILDA. Oh?

EILEEN. How many people know about me and Bob?

HILDA. Just me and your father, Avril—and, of course, the Hadfields.

EILEEN. In that case, how's Bob's wife going to know? She couldn't,
not unless—

HILDA. Yes, dear, not unless somebody told her.

EILEEN. Who'd tell her, then?

HILDA (*slowly*). It could be Mrs. Hadfield.

EILEEN. Mrs. Hadfield? Why?

HILDA. If Avril left Nigel, she might try to blacken our name.

EILEEN (*slowly becoming furious*). Oh? Oh, I've got it now! Oh, I see!
I'm to be the scapegoat, am I—so that dear little Avril can go
hawking her mutton elsewhere!

HILDA. Language, Eileen, language!

EILEEN (*moving* U.L.). I'm going to stay unmarried, am I, for the next
umpteen years, while that sweet little creature in there looks round
for a second husband?

HILDA (*moving* U.R.). It's not that at all, dear. We just want to save your name—and Avril's name—and get everything settled in the nicest possible manner.

EILEEN (*seething*). Very well! I'll settle it for you "in the nicest possible manner". (*She goes to the kitchen door. As she opens it, she calls.*) Avril! (AVRIL *has been listening at the keyhole and stumbles into the room.*) Had a good earful, have you? Right. Get your coat on.

AVRIL. What?

EILEEN. You're going back to Nigel.

AVRIL. Me?

EILEEN. You heard! Get your coat on!

AVRIL. And who do you think you're talking to?

EILEEN. Are you going back to Nigel—or do you want me to drag you back?

AVRIL. Listen to her, Mother. She can't talk to me like that. Me? A married woman? I've got some status, I have.

EILEEN (*sarcastically*). All right, married woman—get back to your husband!

AVRIL. Mother, I'm sorry to hear she's turned out so touchy. If I'd known, I'd have waited— I'd never have got married before her— I'd have waited.

HILDA. Avril!

EILEEN (*about to attack*). Why, you little bitch!

HILDA. Eileen!

AVRIL (*running away from* EILEEN). Hear what she said, Mother? Hear what she called me? You're very lucky this family doesn't disown you—messing about with somebody else's husband!

(HILDA *has dashed to the inter-com phone and is rapidly turning the handle.* EILEEN *and* AVRIL *are now on either side of the settee.*)

HILDA. Dad, can you come up?

EILEEN. You just let me get hold of you—

(*They start moving round the settee,* EILEEN *chasing* AVRIL. *Pandemonium.*)

HILDA (*into phone*). No, it isn't settled!

EILEEN (*threatening*). You just let me—

HILDA. The neighbours, Eileen, the neighbours!

AVRIL (*to* EILEEN). You touch me and I'll scream the place down!

(AVRIL *has picked up a vase.*)

HILDA. Put that down, Avril! Put it down! (*Into phone.*) They've gone out of their minds—your daughters, that's who! Dad, come up! Please! Avril, put it down!

(HILDA *puts the phone down and dashes to get between* AVRIL *and*

EILEEN. *At the same time* TOM *enters from hall, still carrying his best trousers.*)

TOM. Can't one of you women help me with my trousers?

HILDA. I've no time for sewing on buttons.

TOM. It's not a button, it's my zip! What about you, Eileen?

EILEEN. Get out!

TOM. Avril?

AVRIL. Get out!

TOM. Mom?

HILDA. You heard!

TOM. Okee-doke. (TOM *leaves.*)

    (*They are now* D.S.: EILEEN R.; AVRIL C.; HILDA R.C.)

EILEEN. Now look here, Avril!

AVRIL. Now look here, Eileen!

HILDA. Your father will be up in a minute! He'll soon deal with the pair of you!

AVRIL. You tell Dad to keep out of this, Mother. You know how he sides with our Eileen. It isn't fair.

EILEEN (*moves across front stage to* D.L. *Sarcastically*). Oh yes, a fine lot of siding he's been doing with me, hasn't he? Trying to rob me of Bob, that's what he's been doing.

HILDA. You've got the wrong end of the stick, Eileen.

AVRIL. That isn't the only thing she's got the wrong end of, Mother.

EILEEN. Say that again!

HILDA. Just keep that mouth of yours closed, Avril.

AVRIL. What?

HILDA. Keep your tongue still! You're nothing but a little trouble-maker!

AVRIL. Me? A spotless married woman! (*Howls.*) Don't make me throw a fit! Don't make me throw a fit! You know what I'm like when I throw a fit! (*She howls and starts throwing her fit. She kneels on the settee with her head lowered and to* L. *She punches, kicks and yells.*)

HILDA (*moving to* R. *end of settee*). Quiet, Avril! Quiet!

EILEEN. It's all a big act, Mother.

HILDA. Quiet, you, an' all!

    (*Meanwhile* FRED *is hurtled on to the stage in a passenger trolley of the model railway. He hurries through the french windows.*)

FRED. Now then, now then! What's all this on a Sunday morning, day of rest?

    (AVRIL *continues howling.* EILEEN *sits in chair* D.L. *and folds her arms in disgust.*)

HILDA. Shut the French windows, Dad—quick. The sound carries!

FRED. Right, Mother! (*He closes the french windows.*) Shall I draw the curtains as well, to deaden it?

HILDA. Please!

(FRED *does so, then marches towards the front curtains.*)

FRED. What about the front? Shall I draw the front?

HILDA. No, Dad, they might think somebody's dead! (AVRIL *howls.*) Quiet, Avril! Quiet! The neighbours, love!

FRED. Now what's all this pandemonium?

HILDA. They've been acting just like they did when they were children.

FRED. Shut up, Avril—or I'll turn your backside into a patchwork quilt. (AVRIL *stops howling and turns over to lie on her back.*) How's all this started? I thought I left you with a nice, peaceful *dénouement* on your hands.

HILDA. I don't know, Father. It just happened.

FRED (*moving to behind settee*). Well, this is a clear case, isn't it, of "When I lead you not, chaos is come again"—as the Immortal once had it.

HILDA. This is no time for your poetry, Dad.

FRED. It isn't?

HILDA. Our Eileen's gone all cantankerous.

FRED. She's what?

HILDA. She won't make herself amenable—it's most unlike her, but she won't.

FRED (*moving to* EILEEN's *chair*). Oh? So you're indisposed to our proposition, are you?

EILEEN. Yes.

FRED. You are? (*Putting on his formal act.*) What was put to you wasn't put lightly, you know. It was the product of mature thought and careful consideration—as, coming from me, I hope you might expect.

(AVRIL *howls.*)

HILDA. Shut up, Avril! Your father's talking involved. (*To* FRED.) Go on, Father— (*She sits in chair* D.R.)

FRED. Thank you. We all respect you, Eileen—we're all deeply proud of you—and I think I might join up the rest of the family with that remark. (*He glances nervously towards* AVRIL.)

(HILDA *tries to forestall* AVRIL *with:*)

HILDA. Avril—shhh now!

AVRIL (*coming to a sitting position on* C. *of settee*). I didn't say anything.

HILDA (*relieved*). Good.

FRED (*parading up and down*). I know that you have a very shrewd intelligence and so therefore you must have been somewhat mis-informed in the way the terms of our proposition have been pre-sented. Now, if we could go through it all carefully together, you will readily grasp how the benefits of our project are all designed and directed towards your advantage.

HILDA (*thrilled*). He talks to his clients like that! He's a wonderful man.

FRED (*now behind settee* U.R.). Now in the first place, we observe that—

EILEEN (*rising and declaring in lofty, emotional tones to the audience*). I'm sorry, Father, I don't want to listen! I see one single fact: I love a man—I love him.

FRED. All right. I take the point—there's no need to get emotional.

EILEEN. He happens to be unhappily married.

FRED. Unhappily—he happens to be married. Agreed.

EILEEN (*with mounting rhetoric*). I've had to compromise my conscience —I've had to keep matters dark—I've actually lied and deceived—

FRED (*to audience*). Tut-tut-tut.

EILEEN (*with absurd heroics*). I've been as guilty as the rest! And why? Because somewhere I've felt a stupid, sentimental attachment to this family. Well, that's all finished with now. I'm turning my back on you— And do you know something? I suddenly feel clean—pure—chaste!

HILDA (*perplexed*). Chaste?

FRED (*explaining*). They're words they use, Mother. (*With a gesture stressing the emptiness of them.*) Words!

EILEEN (*declamatory*). I'm leaving! I'm going to live with Bob!

FRED. You're what?

HILDA (*rising*). But, Eileen, you can't! Mrs. Hadfield will spread it around that you're the "other woman"!

EILEEN. Let them call me "the other woman"! As long as I've got my integrity, they can call me what they like—concubine, adultress —how about prostitute?

HILDA (*aghast*). Father! We've never had that word in the house!
        (*She staggers into* FRED'S *arms for protection. They remain behind the settee.*)

EILEEN. Well, you've got it now. (*She moves to the hall door.*)

FRED. Eileen, where do you think you're going?

EILEEN. I've told you. I'm leaving with Bob.

HILDA. What will we tell the neighbours?

EILEEN. Tell them I'm living in sin! They'll understand! (*She leaves for upstairs, slamming the door.*)

HILDA. The shame of it—the shame! We'll have to disown her.

FRED. Disown her? We can't disown her, Mother. If we fall out with Eilleen, Bob'll fall out with us—and that'll mean the end of my loco equipment. (*Stoutly.*) Mother!

HILDA. Yes?

FRED (*bravely*). Sacrifices will have to be made.

HILDA. Sacrifices? What sacrifices?

(*They look down at* AVRIL *and then look again at each other with understanding. With strict symmetry,* FRED *walks to* L. *of settee,* HILDA *walks to* R. *Long pause.*)

AVRIL (*alarmed. Looking from one to the other*). Me? Not me!

HILDA. It's very hard on her.

FRED. Very hard.

HILDA. I wouldn't like to go back to Nigel myself.

FRED. Neither would I.

HILDA. But it'd shut Mrs. Hadfield's mouth.

FRED. Exactly.

AVRIL (*frantic*). Dad! He's been unfaithful!

FRED (*feigned tragic*). Sad. But what is man? A weak and wretched creature.

AVRIL (*more frantic*). Dad! I don't love him!

FRED. True. But what is love? A word!

AVRIL (*most frantic*). Dad! He hasn't got any money!

FRED. Ah, there she touches me!

HILDA. Nevertheless, Father, sacrifices must be made.

FRED. Undoubtedly.

HILDA. Go back to him, Avril. Make him your willing slave for life.

FRED. Quite right, Mother. Never forget, Avril, that to err is only human, but to forgive—is bargaining from strength.

AVRIL. I've left him for good and if you try to force me back, I'll have a complete breakdown—and you know what I'm like when I've got my complete breakdown on me.

HILDA. Don't be silly, Avril—don't be silly.

AVRIL. Silly, am I? Do you want a sample? (AVRIL *lowers her head, yells and stamps her feet. At the same time she rubs her fists into her eyes to force the tears. Suddenly she realizes what she is doing. She looks at her fists and walks round to the back of the settee with her head lowered.*)

(*No tears. Slow, tense.*) Mother! Has he made me muck up my mascara?

(*She lifts her head. She has two black eyes.* HILDA *nods.*)

(*Rising. Threatening* FRED.) You just wait till my face is back on.

You just wait! (*She moves into the kitchen.*)

(HILDA *opens the curtains.*)

FRED (*dazed*). As soon as Nigel's mother comes back, we've had it— What's the time? (*He looks at his watch.*) Quarter to twelve! Half time at St. Cuthbert's! Think of her now—down on her benders! I can guess what she's praying about—Nymph in their orisons, all my sins will be remembered, I've no doubt!

(*He wanders to the chair* D.L. *and collapses into it. The following obsessed passages by* FRED *should not be played for laughs. He should be as still as possible and give a feeling of insanity.*)

HILDA. You'll think of something—you always do.

FRED. Think! (*Pause.*) Think? (*With a quiet horror.*) No! Mother!

HILDA. What?

FRED (*slowly*). There are no thoughts. Nothing's coming through. I can't think!

HILDA (*comforting*). Now, Dad—try.

(*During the following* HILDA *fetches the pouffe, places it at the side of* FRED'S *chair and sits beside him.*)

FRED (*dazed, struggling, weak, monotonous tone*). If Avril doesn't go back to Nigel—then Mrs. Hadfield will inform about Bob being married—which will cause Eileen to— (*He breaks off vaguely and says:*) But Eileen's upstairs! And then this afternoon there's the question of my loco— (*In an utterly dazed manner. A quiet madness.*) Loco—loco—loco—

HILDA (*frightened*). Fred! What is it?

FRED (*he grips her*). Mother! (*Pause. They are both quite still.*) It's all become vague—the brain won't march any further— This is the day, Mother. The day I've always dreaded. The brain refuses to fight—it won't fight any more!

HILDA (*whispers*). Father!

FRED. It's with the brain—that's how you trample down the rest; I knew that at school. That's the weapon with which we climb. How have we arrived here in our semi-detached? Only with the brain. What friends have put us here? What capital? What inheritance? It's all been accomplished by this matter which they tell us is grey. Very grey. And now it wants to retire—unpensioned—uninsured.

HILDA. Father, you must rest. Put your head back and rest.

FRED. Rest?

HILDA. You spend too much time all the week worrying—for ever worrying. (*She puts a cushion behind his head.*)

FRED (*frightened*). What will happen—if the brain won't start fighting again? (*Obsessed.*) Strategies, designs, forward-thinking—that's all that's put us here—the working of the wits. They mustn't forsake me, not yet, 'cos you're either climbing up or hanging on. We'll hang on when the time comes—but a little higher up, if you don't mind—a little higher up!

HILDA. That's the way, Father—that's the way.

FRED. Yes, leave me to cogitate, Mother. Let me try to find the way out—philosophically. "Money's the measure of all things"—too true! "I think, therefore I can"—yes, they're both good sayings.

HILDA. Don't get all wound up—just relax.

FRED. "The fear of the law courts is the beginning of wisdom"—most prophetic!

HILDA. Relax and something will come to you—I know it will.

FRED (*nods*). Sudden inspiration—that's what I want—an inward eye-ful! (*He leans his head back on the cushion. He is quite still.*)

   (HILDA *quietly trips away from him and sits on the settee. She stares at him lovingly. She waits.* TOM *enters from the hall, walks round behind the settee until he is beside* FRED.)

TOM. Mother!

HILDA. Shhh!

TOM. What's up?

HILDA. He's having a cogitate, so you mustn't disturb him.

TOM (*looks at* FRED *and grimaces*). That's painful, I bet.

HILDA. Leave him in peace, Thomas! What is it you want, anyway?

TOM. Here, you do 'em, Mother, will you?

HILDA. What?

TOM. My trousers. It won't take you five minutes.

HILDA. Give them here, then—but be quiet. What's wrong with them?

TOM. The zip fastener's stuck. One of the teeth's missing.

HILDA. In that case, it's impossible.

TOM. Eh?

HILDA. Where can I get another zip fastener on a Sunday morning?

TOM (*he produces a bundle of zip fasteners*). Here. Zip fasteners specially selected.

HILDA. Where did you get these?

TOM (*sitting on settee to* HILDA'S L.). A sort-of farewell present from the late-lamented girl-friend. Well, she happened to whip 'em from the works, like.

HILDA. She what?

TOM. She used to work in our zip fastener extension, Mom.

FRED (*dazed*). Zip fastener extension?

TOM. What's up, Dad? Coming round, are you?

FRED (*rising*). Zip fastener extension? Did you say zip fastener extension?

TOM. That's right—zip fastener extension.

FRED (*he dances across to stage* R. *in fantastic glee*). Oh-hoh! Zip fastener extension! Zip fastener extension, eh? Zip fastener extension!

TOM. What's up with Dad?

FRED (*he dances back again to stage* L.). Ha-ha! Ha-ha, ha-ha, ha-hah!

TOM (*quickly*). What's up with him?

FRED. Mother, last time you searched my son's pockets, you came across a letter simply seething with passion?

TOM. You searched my pockets!

FRED. She did—and what she found was the most venerous venery I've ever read in all my natural! (*To* HILDA.) And what was the name of this sweet young baggage—can you remember, Mother?

HILDA. Daphne—that was her name.

FRED. And would Daphne and your zip fastener friend be one and the same?

TOM. What are you getting at?

FRED. There isn't more than one Daphne in the zip fastener department by any chance?

TOM (*stammers*). Well, no.

FRED. So it's right what me and your mother have suspected all along?

TOM. What's that?

FRED (*at* L. *end of sofa*). In plain terms, you have put a young lady in the club. Have you or haven't you?

TOM. Well, sort-of.

FRED. There's no sort-of about the club!

TOM. All right, I have, then. How do you know?

FRED. Deduction, lad.

HILDA. He's done what?

FRED. Leave us, Mother, leave us. It's a very tender moment, this. (*To* TOM.) Let's savour it together, father and son—alone. Mother—leave us.

(HILDA *rises and moves to the door. She turns.*)

HILDA (*bewildered*). Can't you explain? I don't know what to make of it— What club, Fred?

(FRED *ushers her into the kitchen-dinette and closes the door on her. He moves round* TOM, *who is still seated.*)

FRED (*feigned grief*). What made you do it? What made you?

TOM. Well, it was raining at the time—and she got under my mac—and it hardly fits me—and—

FRED. No, not that— What made you force her into another man's arms?

TOM. Oh—well, once I knew she'd clicked, I said to myself, "What would my father do in this situation"?

FRED. You what?

TOM. So I did it.

FRED. You palmed her off on Nigel's uncle, Mr. Makepiece?

TOM. Yes.

FRED. Oh dear! Oh dear! How it comes home to roost! My methods should never be applied by amateurs—never!

TOM. Did I do wrong, then?

FRED (*to audience*). "Wrong," he says! "Did I do wrong?" You've done worse than wrong—you've ruined everybody's bank balance!

TOM. Me?

FRED. Because of your little hanky-pank, Nigel's been cut off.

TOM. What?

FRED. Mr. Makepiece has cut him out of his will in favour of this future bride you're giving him.

TOM. He has?

FRED. That alone would be enough. But to think you've consolidated the situation by providing him with his future heir! (*Raising his voice.*) Most considerate towards your family you've been, I must say! (*Shouts.*) Idiot! Fool! Bungler!

(HILDA *rushes in from the kitchen.*)

HILDA. Dad! What's the noise? Has he disgraced us completely—is that it? I said he'd be the one to let us down. (*Shouts.*) How could you, Tom? How could you?

(EILEEN *rushes in from the hall.*)

EILEEN. Father!

FRED. Yes?

EILEEN. I'm just going.

FRED. Going?

(BOB *dashes in through the french windows, shouting:*)

BOB. We'll never get it up the track this afternoon—King George the Fifth has sprung another leak!

(AVRIL *rushes in from the kitchen and shouts:*)

AVRIL. Just tell me once and for all— Am I going to get my divorce or aren't I? Well?

(Simultaneously)

(*Together, shouting and moving from one to another. Turmoil.*)

EILEEN (*to* BOB). Now look here, Bob, this is the last opportunity I'm giving you of putting locomotives out of your mind and deciding whether you love me or not. Come on! (*Threatening.*) What's your answer going to be, because if you don't—

BOB (*to* FRED). The flux simply won't stick to the union pipe! I've got it absolutely clean, but it still won't stick. I bet any money it's the electric iron. (*Shouts.*) I said, "Something's wrong with the electric iron". Have you had trouble with your element at all? What else can it be if it isn't the temperature of the iron?

TOM (*to* HILDA). I didn't know, Mother, honestly I didn't. I never gave it a thought that he might cut Nigel off. I mean, what was I to do when she told me she was expecting? I didn't want to bring scandal on the family or anything of the kind—

AVRIL (*to* HILDA *and* FRED). The way I've been treated in this house this morning is enough to give me a nervous breakdown. Me! A married woman with my husband unfaithful. And do you think I get any sympathy from my parents? Well, I tell you this: if you try to stop me having that divorce, there's plenty of beans I'll be spilling—

HILDA (*from one to another*). Eileen, do be quiet— Well, yes, I know you're sorry, Tom— Avril! Keep your voice down! Not so loud, Bob! Not so loud—the neighbours! For Heaven's sake not so much noise. Eileen, now, please! Tom! Avril! Bob! The neighbours! Don't forget the neighbours!

(*During the above uproar* FRED *walks towards the fourth wall which divides the two houses. He reaches front stage* C. *He stares towards the audience. Suddenly there is a look of horror on his face. Without turning round he roars:*)

FRED. Silence!

(*Everyone is silent. From the fourth wall comes the sound of tapping.*)

HILDA (*with whispered horror*). Dad!

(*The tapping is repeated.*)

FRED (*bringing up his right hand to strike his heart and staring open-eyed into the audience*). They're knocking on the wall!

(*The tapping is repeated.* HILDA *moves to* FRED'S *side at front* C. *stage. During the following they do not look at each other, but stare glassy-eyed into the audience.*)

HILDA. The neighbours! This is the end— They'll find out— We'll be ruined.

(*Almost mechanically* FRED'S *hand grips hers.*)

FRED. Have courage, Mother! I promise you a solution— As long
as we can keep them quiet.

(*The tapping is repeated.*)

HILDA. We mustn't let them think we've been quarrelling.

FRED. No. Let them think we've been having a party— That's it!
A family party! A happy family party! We must laugh! Come on!
Let 'em hear us laughing! Come on, Mother! Laugh! Everybody
laugh!

*They all line up at front of stage and stand absolutely still like
dummies. Their positions are symmetrical. They laugh at the fourth
wall.*

*The louder their volume of laughter, the louder becomes the tapping.
As each side struggles for victory,*

THE CURTAIN FALLS.

ACT THREE

As the house lights are lowered, we hear the insistent tapping once again. It seems to come from in front of the curtain. It stops abruptly.

The curtain rises.

The characters are standing in the same positions as they were at the end of Act Two. They are equidistant from each other, as if taking a curtain call, with HILDA and FRED in the centre. They are still laughing.)

HILDA. It's stopped.

FRED. Splendid.

(*They stop laughing.* FRED *takes a step forward and marches to* D.R.)

(*As if addressing a platoon.*) Let that be a lesson to the lot of you—Now let's have a bit of strict rotation about it, shall we? Bob!

BOB. Yes, Mr. Midway? . .

FRED. Try and do the best you can with King George the Fifth. If you can't, we'll have to retire him.

BOB. Right you are, Mr. Midway. (*He leaves through the french windows.*)

FRED. Avril!

AVRIL. Yes, Dad?

FRED. Haven't you had your Eskimo Nell Deep-Freeze Sponge-cake yet?

AVRIL. Now look, Dad—

FRED (*overriding her*). Your mother bought one specially at the Supermarket yesterday, knowing you were coming and your partiality for it.

AVRIL. She did?

FRED (*to* HILDA). Into action, Mother! Give her an extra large slice. Fill her mouth up!

(HILDA *bundles her into the kitchen.*)

Eileen!

EILEEN. Now don't try any of your funny stuff, Dad; it won't work. I'm going to the Dragon Hotel—and Bob's coming with me.

FRED. The Dragon Hotel?

EILEEN. Yes.

FRED. Then you'd better get your case packed.

EILEEN. All right! I will! (*She stalks out of the door into the hall.*)

(FRED *moves* U.R. *following her to the door.* TOM *is creeping across the room to the french window as* FRED *turns.*)

FRED. And where are you going?

TOM. I thought you wanted the room to yourself.

FRED. Sit down! You and me haven't finished, not by a long chalk. (TOM *sits on the pouffe* L. *He is crouched and sheepish.*) (*Approaching him. Emotionally.*) My poor, dear, offspring! Why didn't you tell me? Why didn't you? I'd have understood. I'm a man of the world. These misfortunes happen to a young fellow. (*His manner changes abruptly and he clips his son over the head.*) All right, let's have the full story!

TOM. Well, the very first moment she thought she'd clicked, I advised her to head for Mr. Makepiece—and she's a very fast worker who'll never take "No" for an answer.

FRED (*amazed*). You actually forced her into another man's arms?

TOM. I was only thinking of what was best for her. I mean—I haven't got a lot to offer at the moment, have I—and then I suddenly remembered the technique you employed in getting our Avril married to Nigel.

FRED (*bursts*). You what?

TOM. Well, you did get her to—er—compromise him up a bit, didn't you?

FRED (*bursts*). Thomas! It's natural for a man to be ambitious for his daughter—but not for his consort. Even I draw the line at that! (*Probing.*) Nevertheless, I expect she's had quite an increase in pay in her—new job?

TOM. Well, yes, she has.

FRED (*probing*). And I imagine she's a girl of very generous inclinations —not only physical but financial.

TOM (*frightened*). I—don't quite follow.

FRED (*sarcastically*). Don't you indeed— Where exactly did you get the money for that new motor-bike of yours?

TOM. Well, I—er—

FRED. The facts! Give me the facts!

TOM. Well, actually, when she told Mr. Makepiece she was expecting, he gave her a certain sum of money—and she lent it to me.

FRED (*staggered, he claps his hand to his forehead*). Living off immoral earnings on top! (*Reeling across front of stage.*) You disgust me! You appal me! You horrible juvenile delinquent!

TOM (*rising*). Look, Dad, I'm only nineteen. I'm not ready for marriage—not yet!

FRED. Not ready for marriage!

TOM. I'm still a teenager!

FRED. My son—a teenage Pandarus and apparently proud of it! Sit down!

(TOM *sits. Long pause.*)

TOM (*half rising*). But Dad—

FRED. Shut up!

(TOM *sits again, huddled and guilt-ridden.* FRED, *not knowing what to say, walks* U.S. *He arrives at the rear wall* L., *almost face to face with one of Tretchikoff's pictures of a coloured girl. It inspires him. He looks at the picture, then at his son, then at the picture again. He turns.*)

Do you know how a young lad becomes an adult in the African bush?

TOM. I've never thought about it.

FRED. Well, I have. It was in my correspondence course of "Facts that will Astound your Colleagues". (*Pause.*) In the African bush, they take a lad of twelve or thirteen, perform a minor surgical operation and say, "Right, mate, from now on you're a fully signed-up member of the tribe, so act responsible—or else! In return for the benefits what accrue, you'll obey its laws and do your proper share of hunting". (*Pause. Sympathetically. Moving to* L. *of settee.*) That's why I can't really blame you, son. You see, in our fair civilization we've actually encouraged you in irresponsibility.

TOM. You've what?

FRED. If we don't give you real responsibility, what can you do but be irresponsible? (*Moving to* D.R.) What I'd like to offer you, lad, is real adventure, real life adventure.

TOM. Oh?

FRED (*rapidly*). One wife, two kids, three rooms, the landlord knocking at the door and the insurance man about to call. (*Taking a cigar from his pocket and moving to* TOM.) So, lad, from this moment onwards, I declare you adult! (*He stuffs the cigar in* TOM'S *mouth.*) That means you've got to lie, scrounge and deceive with the rest of us—but never put yourself in a position where anybody can accuse you of it— Now, your first act is to get yourself married.

(FRED *moves towards the telephone* R., *but stops short* C. *on his way to it when* TOM *says:*)

TOM. But what about the money?

FRED (*entranced.* C. *to audience*). "What about the money?" What splendid first words to come from an initiate's lips! (*To* TOM.) Don't worry. You're in a privileged position.

(*He picks up the phone book and looks through it. It is on the window table* R.)

TOM. What are you doing?

FRED. Simply acting on your behalf as one of the co-directors of this basic limited company of ours, the family. (*While he dials.*) Don't look alarmed, Thomas. You can call me Fred from now on if you wish. (TOM *lights the cigar and continues sitting* L., *smoking it in a highly delighted and self-satisfied manner.* FRED, *into phone.*) 'morning, Mr. Makepiece—Midway here—Midway! My daughter married your nephew—that's right— No, it's nothing to do with Nigel— No, it actually concerns my son, my son Thomas. I thought you might be able to help me— It appears he's been jilted by a young lady called Daphne, who used to work in your zip fastener department—He tells me you—er—happen to know her—I wonder if you'd be kind enough to help? I've been holding him back from the gas oven all morning. Well, the fact of the matter is—he's a very shy lad who's been nourishing a burning passion—the poor child even imagined he might marry her —What? You'll come round immediately? Oh no, we wouldn't impose—not on a Sunday. Perhaps if you told him over the phone that you're going to make her very happy, perhaps that might suffice— He's rung off! (*He taps the button.*) Rung off! What a marvellous hurry he must be in to get here! (*Imagining it.*) Think of him now, jumping into his three-litre and slamming the door! (*Pause. Then briskly.*) Right! Stage one accomplished. (*He bangs down the receiver and marches to the kitchen door.*) Stage two coming up. (*He opens the door and shouts.*) Mother!

HILDA (*enters*). Yes, dear?

FRED. Your little boy has now become a man.

HILDA. You mean it's right what you said, then—he's going to become a father?

FRED (*rapidly*). At-a-top-secret-and-most-unofficial-level-which-I-hope-we'll-all-keep-under-our-hats-perhaps-we-might-safely-say—he is.

HILDA (*romantically moving down to* R. *of* TOM). My son a father!

FRED (*slightly irritated, bounds round settee to* R.C.). Nobody's to know as yet.

HILDA (*moving to* C.). Who's the lucky girl? This Daphne Dunmore, is it?

FRED (*curt*). Yes, but we must forget it at the moment.

HILDA. Is she up to his standard, do you think?

FRED. She will be—if you keep your mouth shut.

HILDA. He'll marry her, then?

FRED (*frantic*). Yes, but we're not supposed to know!

HILDA. When will it be—the marriage?

FRED. Mother! Shut up!

HILDA. Shut up?

FRED. Yes, shut up— (*Puts his arm round her, tenderly.*) Do you trust me, my dearest?

HILDA. You know I do.

FRED. This is the way we're going to play it for our public image. Right then! (*He sits HILDA on the settee and motions TOM to stand.*) There stands our son who's never had an unclean thought in his life.

HILDA (*puzzled. Looking up at FRED*). He hasn't?

(FRED *shakes his head, looking at* HILDA, *then refers to his son.*)

FRED. Agreed, Thomas?

TOM. As you say—Fred.

FRED. One day, wandering through the zip fastener room, he came across Daphne and they shyly smiled at each other.

HILDA (*puzzled*). He did?

(FRED *nods his head, looking at* HILDA, *then refers to his son.*)

FRED. Agreed, Thomas?

TOM. As you say, Fred.

FRED (*in full flight of lyricism*). Days passed, weeks passed, months passed, and then one morning in spring he summoned up enough courage and asked her to walk with him in the woods. They walked and they walked and they walked, and he never so much as touched her hand.

HILDA (*puzzled*). He didn't?

(FRED *shakes his head, looking at* HILDA, *then refers to his son.*)

FRED. Agreed, Thomas?

TOM. As you say, Fred.

FRED. The very next day she was lured away by Mr. Makepiece. (*Sadly.*) Ever since then, the poor lad—with his purity hanging heavy on him—has been wrapped in a frustration which has slowly turned his brain.

HILDA (*puzzled*). It has?

(FRED *nods his head and is about to say, "Agreed, Thomas?" when* HILDA *asks:*)

Well, how did he put her in the family way, then?

FRED. Mother, I've just been describing our strategy.

HILDA. You mean all that nice stuff about purity and his walk through the woods isn't the truth?

FRED (*crossing to* L. *of settee*). Of course it isn't the truth!

HILDA. What is the truth, then?

FRED (*pained*). Mother, surely you should know by this time—truth is something you keep to yourself. What we've just been describing is my son's public image which I sincerely hope you and him will be able to keep up for the next half-hour at least.

HILDA. Why?

FRED. Because Mr. Makepiece is coming.

HILDA. Mr. Makepiece?

FRED. Mr. Makepiece thinks he is the father of that lad's child.

HILDA. He does?

FRED. By courtesy of Daphne, of course.

HILDA. Oh, I see it all now!

FRED. Splendid! Anyway, leave everything to me when he arrives. Thomas!

TOM. Yes, Fred.

FRED. If you're going to act like Parsifal the Pure, you'd better get tidied up.

TOM (*moving to hall door*). Right, Fred.

FRED. And you'd better not call me Fred in front of Mr. Makepiece.

TOM. O.K., Fred. (*He leaves by the hall door.*)

HILDA. Why is he calling you Fred?

FRED. I've just matured him up to man's estate, so I've given him the privilege as a token thereof.

HILDA (*rising*). Well, I just can't keep up with it. (*Moves to* L. *and places pouffe at* R. *of chair.*) You know, I'd say this is one of the busiest Sunday mornings we've had for a long time.

(HILDA *starts dusting the books and gramophone records on shelves* D.L. FRED *moves up to* U.R. *of settee.* EILEEN *enters and without saying a word walks round the room picking up pieces of her property. She takes the framed picture by Tretchikoff from the wall, then to her mother's surprise she takes out of her hands the gramophone record she is dusting.* EILEEN *continues round the room, picking up a small clock, an ash tray, a cigarette box and a ceramic figure of a cat with a long neck. She is about to leave when:*)

FRED. And what do you think you're doing?

EILEEN. They're all mine. I bought them.

HILDA. You're not really packing?

EILEEN. I'm not staying here.

HILDA. Where are you going to?

EILEEN. I've told you: the Dragon Hotel—with Bob. (*She leaves through hall door.*)

HILDA (*moves to behind settee*). If she stays there with a married man, you'll have to disown her—there's no two ways about it.

FRED. Disown my Eileen? We'll have to try and keep her here, then.

HILDA (*sarcastically*). How are you going to do that—tie her down?

FRED (*moves* D.L., *trying to work it out.* HILDA *moves to chair* R. *and sits*). It's all very tricky—if we lose Eileen, we lose Bob—if we lose Bob, I lose my locos and I'm back where I started. (*Pause. Then excitedly.*) Wait a minute! Wait a minute!

HILDA (*expectantly*). Yes, Dad?

FRED (*bounds back to* C.). Dear-oh-dear! I've just been hit by a piece of Eureka! I'm sure of it! Yes—yes— It all fits together!

HILDA. What is it, Dad?

FRED. Why not ask Bob to come and live here?

HILDA. Bob live here?

FRED. It's simple! Bob lives here and Eileen lives with him!

HILDA. You mean having 'em living in sin—here—under our own roof?

FRED. But don't you see this is the only place where we can make it completely respectable! Who would believe that a decent family like ours could possibly connive at such immorality? We'll say the reason we invited him to stay was to keep an eye on him.

HILDA (*entranced*). We become sort of Guardians of their Decency?

FRED. Exactly, Mother. (*Throwing away to audience.*) As long as he has a bed down here—and she has a bed up there—who are we to worry about a few creaks on the stairs in the dead of night?

HILDA. I believe you're right, Father—I believe you're absolutely right.

FRED (*sentimentally*). Look, Mother, I must confess, I'm fonder of our Eileen than I am of our other children. She's my favourite, so do help me bring her back to the fold, won't you?

HILDA. How can I do that?

FRED. Ask Bob if he'll stay here— After all, he's the bait where our Eileen's concerned. However much she loves honesty, it can't stop her being thirty next birthday, can it?

HILDA. You're right.

FRED. Ask Bob to stay, then. (*Flattering her.*) And do it warm and motherly, as you alone know how.

HILDA. Shall I ask him now?

FRED (*puts his arm round her and leads her to the french window*). Yes. And tell him to pass the news on to Eileen. She'd appreciate it coming from him—just as he'd appreciate it coming from you.

HILDA. Where is he?

FRED. Down in the workshop. Where do you think?

HILDA. Very well, love. Leave it to me. (*She leaves by the french windows.*)

    (FRED *pauses for a moment and then calls* AVRIL *out of the kitchen.*)

FRED. Avril!

    (AVRIL *enters.*)

(*Moving to settee and sitting down on* R. *end.*) Avril, my little one—I have just phoned Mr. Makepiece and told him of your marital rift.

AVRIL (*now behind* L. *end of settee*). You've what?

FRED. He told me he'd come straight over.

AVRIL (*amazed*). Nigel's uncle coming here?

FRED. To try and seal the rift.

AVRIL. You mean he'll put Nigel back in the will?

FRED. More than likely, dear—more than likely. But I say to myself: surely there's a moral issue here. I can't have my daughter return to him just for the money.

AVRIL. I wouldn't mind.

FRED. Never! The man has behaved like a dirty beast. Think of that!

AVRIL (*perches on* L. *arm of the settee*). Well, as a matter of fact, Dad, I've been thinking about it.

FRED. You have?

AVRIL. I think he might have certain depths he's never tapped. Well, not with me, anyway.

FRED. Oh yes, he's got those all right.

AVRIL. Do you think he might be a late-developer or something? (*Holding her father's arm.*) Father, if I went back to him, what should be my approach?

FRED (*embarrassed*). Details like that are not for me to say.

AVRIL. Not even a little hint?

FRED. Well, I— er—

AVRIL. Yes?

FRED. I should buy yourself a sound, practical correspondence course on the subject.

    (NIGEL *walks up to the front door and rings the chimes.*)

AVRIL (*moving towards front window*). Who's that?

FRED (*prevents her and leads her towards the kitchen*). Keep away from the window. It's probably Mr. Makepiece. You'd better make yourself scarce in the kitchen-dinette.

AVRIL. I'm sick of the kitchen-dinette.

FRED (*pushing her in and shutting the door*). So am I—but get in there!

    (FRED *goes into the hall, and opens the front door. We hear him say disappointedly, "Oh, it's you." He returns with* NIGEL.)

NIGEL (U.R.). Mother's sent me ahead in the car to collect Avril. She says there won't be any difficulty about it.

FRED (at NIGEL's L.). Indeed!

NIGEL. Mother says she's no wish to cross your threshold or even communicate with this family again unless she is forced to—and Avril and I have got to shake the dust off our feet as well.

FRED. Citing Scripture for her purpose? Not the first by no means.

NIGEL. She's walking this way—and she says there'll be Halifax to pay if I haven't got hold of Avril before she gets here.

FRED. How long will it take her? Ten minutes?

NIGEL. About that.

FRED (briskly). Right! (Puts his arm across NIGEL's shoulders and leads him to C.) I've got some good news for you—I've been in touch with your uncle.

NIGEL. My uncle?

FRED. A splendid, generous, kindly man, your uncle. Think of all what he's given to Dowlihull: a church tower, two public lavatories and a garden of rest—and they still keep him waiting for his O.B.E.

There's no justice! I told him that being cut out of the will was such a shock to a nephew's heart that it led you to your dire debauchery and present misfortune.

NIGEL. You know, I never thought of making up anything like that.

FRED. Well, I have—and he's coming round here.

NIGEL. Coming round here—my uncle? Do you think he might put me back in the will?

FRED. Most likely—most likely.

NIGEL (moving towards hall door). I must go and find Mother!

FRED. Wait! Shouldn't you break the news to your wife first?

NIGEL (returning). You mean—Avril will be coming back to me?

FRED. A word of advice before you see her. (He motions NIGEL to sit down on the settee, then joins him.) Have you ever tried to understand our Avril—or simply a woman, for that matter—with all her mysteries and complications?

NIGEL. Well, actually, I must admit I did once look at some diagrams.

FRED. I'm talking about a woman's heart—her mental make-up.

NIGEL. Oh?

FRED. Do you realize what she feels like when she knows that your rich, virile, authentic, savage passion has been denied her—that you've actually spent it elsewhere?

NIGEL. Oh!

FRED. What heart-searchings she must have of her own deficiency! What inferiority! What frustration! You must gird up your loins, my son. Go to her! And give her the reassurance she requires! She's there—waiting—in the kitchen-dinette. Need I say more?
(NIGEL *rises and walks to the door, but turns.*)

NIGEL. Does that mean I ought to tell her the truth?

FRED. The truth? (*Pause.*) That's a most suspicious word, the truth. Here, come back. Old Jesting Pilate wants another word with you. (NIGEL *sits down again.*) There's something else on your mind, isn't there, Nigel?

NIGEL. Well, yes.

FRED. Tell your dear father-in-law. He can bear all.

NIGEL. Well, when I went into this room—in London—with this woman—

FRED. The room in London with the woman—yes?

NIGEL. Nothing happened.

FRED (*amazed*). Nothing happened?

NIGEL. I suddenly felt wicked and frightened inside—and between ourselves, I didn't quite feel up to it in any case.

FRED. You what?

NIGEL. I paid her the money and waited till Tommy Hickerton was ready next door.

FRED. But why didn't you tell Avril?

NIGEL. I was going to—but I got as far as where I climbed up the stairs—and then I blushed. Avril jumped to conclusions and bolted out of the house. I haven't seen her alone since then.

FRED. Why haven't you told Mrs. Hadfield, then?

NIGEL. I say, Mr. Midway, it isn't quite the kind of thing a fellow discusses with his mother!

FRED (*rises and moves* U.R. *Enraged*). So because you blushed, we've had all this blasted havoc on a Sunday morning, have we?

NIGEL. I'm sorry if there's been any inconvenience (*Rises.*)—but I think if I go and tell Avril the truth now, everything will be nicely cleared up. (*He walks to the kitchen door.*)

FRED. Here! Here! Here! Not so fast, not so fast!

NIGEL. What is it? .

FRED (*moving to* NIGEL). My daughter's waiting for the Mr. Hyde, the Don Juan to appear—and here you are acting like a bowdlerized version of the Virgin's Lament. Sit down!

NIGEL. What again?

FRED. Again!

(NIGEL *sits on settee.*)

(U.R. *of settee.*) Do you realize my daughter's in there all wound-up ready to meet the challenge of your new-found, hot-blooded, voluptuous dimension! Think of her disappointment and dis-illusionment if all she finds you can offer her is your old original, lymphatic self! It's enough to give the poor child a dose of the neurotic hab-dabs.

NIGEL. You mean she'll scream?

FRED. Exactly.

NIGEL. I can't bear it when she screams.

FRED. Neither can I— There's only one thing we can do.

NIGEL. What's that?

FRED. You've established yourself as a dirty beast—you'd better stay a dirty beast.

NIGEL. You think so?

FRED. I'm sure of it, lad. It'll avoid any more complications.

NIGEL. Well, how do I go about it, then?

FRED. Looking at you, that's the difficulty. (*Picking up a Sunday newspaper from table behind settee and giving it to* NIGEL.) Here, read this from cover to cover every Sunday—and use your imagination for the rest of the week! Go and sit outside among the birds and the bees and get cracking.

NIGEL (*rising and moving to french windows*). Very well, Mr. Midway. (*He leaves for the garden.*)

(FRED *moves to the front window and looks out.*)

FRED. The moment has arrived! He's here! "Deus ex three-litre!"

(MAKEPIECE *moves to the front door while* FRED *goes into the hall to let him in. They both move into the living-room.* MAKEPIECE *is between fifty-five and sixty. He is dressed in a well-cut suit.*)

MAKEPIECE (*entering*). Now let me warn you, Midway, time is precious. I'm a very busy man.

FRED (*entering*). Aren't we all, Mr. Makepiece—aren't we all?

(MAKEPIECE *moves to* L. *end of settee.* FRED *moves to* R. *end.*)

MAKEPIECE. You say there's some kind of emotional disturbance in your family and I might be able to help.

FRED. Yes, that's about it.

MAKEPIECE. You say it concerns your son and a young lady named—er—Daphne, both of whom work for me.

FRED. That's it. Do sit down.

MAKEPIECE. Er—thank you. (*But he doesn't. He starts walking to and fro pompously with his hands behind his back.*) As you might realize,

I have frequently spoken about the responsibility which falls upon me for happiness and contentment among my workers.

FRED. And beautifully reported in the *Dowlihull Weekly News,* I might say.

MAKEPIECE. Er—yes. So if there is anything I can do to heal the breach between your son and this—er—Daphne, so that I can see them safely—or rather, happily—married, you have only to say the word. (*He sits in chair* L.)

FRED (*very politely*). May I speak?

MAKEPIECE. You may.

(FRED *now walks about pompously with his hands behind his back.*)

FRED. We are, as you see, Mr. Makepiece, very simple souls in a semi-detached. But to get to our present position we have had to try and emulate, however gropingly, some standard or some norm. I think I speak on behalf of a million others when I say that the ideal which we try to achieve is something like you, Mr. Makepiece.

MAKEPIECE. You flatter me.

FRED. Not in the least. But you must realize it is impossible for us, the disciples, to allow our hero to have feet of clay. We must try to cover up his deficiencies for him. With the proviso that he who covers up most should merit the best chance of promotion.

MAKEPIECE. That's what I usually call the rewards of loyalty.

FRED. Exactly, Mr. Makepiece. Consequently, it would be as distasteful for me as it would be for you to talk at length about this—er—Daphne and her—er—progeny. I think we might agree that a little money might render the problem as it confronts both you and us—how shall I say—insignificant. (*He sits on chair* R.)

MAKEPIECE. My turn?

FRED. Your turn.

MAKEPIECE. Let's drop the verbal fencing, shall we?

FRED. Right! (*He dashes across stage and sits on the pouffe at* MAKE-PIECE'S *right.*)

MAKEPIECE (*confidentially*). Obviously you know that women, especially vivacious ones, have an undeniable attraction for me. I believe every fresh courtship regenerates youth—keeps the blood circulating—the heart in trim. Nevertheless, Daphne with her quaint infatuation for me has certainly become an embarrassment. I agree with you; she needs a young man nearer her own age. Furthermore, to commit myself to a child of her tender years and—er—background at this particular point in time could have most unfortunate consequences. (*Rises and moves to* D.C.) As a sympathetic disciple, you may know that, as rumour has it, I am short-listed for an O.B.E. in the coming year.

FRED (*rises and moves to* L. *of* MAKEPIECE). And may I say the whole of Dowlihull is delighted to hear it?

MAKEPIECE. It is?

FRED. Oh, yes, I've heard talk in the loco club that it might even be a knighthood.

MAKEPIECE. A knighthood? Oh no, no, no. No, as a matter of fact, I think in the end it will only be an M.B.E.

FRED (*amazed and springing to his defence*). What? You, Mr. Makepiece? Palm you off with an M.B.E.? Oh dear, if they try to do that across you, I should send it back.

MAKEPIECE (*muses*). You really think it might be a knighthood?

FRED. To my mind, there's only one thing that stands in your way.

MAKEPIECE. This—er—Miss Daphne?

FRED. Exactly. I think the evidence shows that any blatant moral discrepancies should always appear after rather than before the reception of the accolade. Any display of immorality before would be *lèse-majesté*—and so you wouldn't get it—but after, it would simply mean you're following in the tradition of our glorious noble inheritance.

MAKEPIECE. My view entirely.

FRED. So if I, your disciple, were to persuade my son to cover up any —er—moral deviationism on your part, I take it my son-in-law, your nephew, would then be reinstated as your heir.

MAKEPIECE. He would.

FRED. May I make a suggestion?

MAKEPIECE. Please do.

FRED. I think perhaps if you were to found an Overseas Scholarship or say Bursary to encourage your young workers to travel abroad and seek experience—and if it were awarded this first year to my son—I think he would get married to—er—Daphne, go abroad with her and, depending on the sum—never come back again.

MAKEPIECE. And what would be the sum?

FRED. X pounds.

MAKEPIECE. And what is X pounds?

FRED. X pounds, as you know, is a business expression. It means it's not very nice to talk about it, but your listener must imagine it's as high as possible. How high can you imagine, Mr. Makepiece? Remember, if you do it in the form of a covenant, there'll be no Income Tax. So your X sixpences will be miraculously transformed into my son's X pounds. And the world will justly say, "Is there no

end to his beneficence?" That'll put you straight in line for the
(*With a gesture*)—tap on the shoulder. Top status! I'm tempted to
call you "Sir Arnold" already.

MAKEPIECE. You touch me. Put it there, Midway. I'm proud to
know you.

(They shake hands.)

FRED. Would you like to meet the young man in question?

MAKEPIECE. I don't think there's any need. Matters can quite easily
be settled between us—

(HILDA enters from the garden with BOB.)

HILDA. Mr. Makepiece, is it?

(FRED moves U.S. while HILDA comes down to shake hands.)

MAKEPIECE. Your good lady? Happy to meet you.

(She shakes hands and moves to chair R. and sits.)

FRED. This is Bob—helps me with the locos.

MAKEPIECE. I've heard about your locos.

(BOB attempts to come D.S. to shake hands with MAKEPIECE. But FRED prevents it by shaking hands with BOB himself. At the same time he ushers BOB D.L.)

FRED. I'd like you to have a look at them before you go.

MAKEPIECE. You would?

FRED *(moving to MAKEPIECE and ushering him to the french window)*. If
you'd care to step out into the garden, Mr. Makepiece, I'll be with
you in a moment—and then we can wind up our discussion.

MAKEPIECE. But I thought we had wound it up.

FRED. Oh no. We haven't yet got to the exciting part.

MAKEPIECE. What's that?

FRED. What X equals— Just along the path—you'll see the shed at
the bottom.

MAKEPIECE. Thank you. *(He moves off.)*

FRED *(bounding back to C.)*. It's all working out beautifully, Mother!
Beautifully! *(To BOB.)* Now then, Bob, has Mother explained the
situation to you?

BOB *(moving to L.C.)*. She has!

FRED. And you're coming to live here?

BOB. I think it's a marvellous idea—I can be closer to the locos.

FRED. And Eileen. You mustn't forget Eileen, too.

BOB. Oh well, I take Eileen for granted.

FRED. Take Eileen for granted? *(Moving close to BOB.)* Look, get this
into your head: you're coming here primarily as Eileen's lover in
sheep's clothing—not as a means of advertising your firm.

BOB. Naturally. But it's part and parcel of the same thing, isn't it?

I mean—coming here, you'll want me to work on the locos as well as on Eileen, won't you?

FRED. My influence has been too great! You're beginning to worry me. (*Moving to hall door and opening it.*) Do you know that? Worry me! Get up them stairs and break the news to Eileen. (BOB *moves to the doorway.*) She's got something to offer you, lad, what I haven't—so get up there! (*He closes the door on* BOB.)

(NIGEL *calls from the garden and moves on stage.*)

NIGEL. Mr. Midway! Mr. Midway!

FRED. Yes?

NIGEL (*moving to the kitchen door*). I've just seen uncle in the garden and he tells me I'm going back in the will. I must tell Avril.

FRED. How have you got on with your Sunday reading?

NIGEL. Oh, I've read a case here—and you'd be surprised what ideas it's put in my head. I feel inspired—I really do. Could I go in and see her?

FRED. Why not? With your inspiration in one hand and your money in the other—what else can a good husband offer?

(NIGEL *opens the door and walks in boldly.*)

(*Calls after him.*) Be careful of the crockery, won't you? Keep to the dinette rather than the kitchen. (*He closes the door on him.*) There you are, Mother, another set of customers is satisfied— (*Smiles contentedly.*) Well, now, one short chat with Mr. Makepiece over finance and everything will be settled all round. (*He goes into the garden.*)

HILDA (*rises and exclaims admiringly*). A marvellous man!

(BOB *and* EILEEN *enter from the hall.* EILEEN *moves to* R.C. BOB *moves* U.L.)

(*With a coy giggle.*) Here they come, the lovebirds. (*To* BOB.) Have you told her yet?

BOB. I'm just explaining it.

HILDA. I'll let you get on with it, then. (*Giggles and touches* EILEEN.) Soon we'll have you both cooing under our roof. (*Romantically.*) The lovebirds! (*She leaves through the door to the hall.*)

BOB. Well, Eileen?

EILEEN. You're not staying here.

BOB (*moving to* L.C.). But your mother's right; it's the best way all round.

EILEEN. I've heard the argument—but you're not staying!

BOB. Who says so?

EILEEN (*moving* U.R.). I say so.

BOB. Eileen, let's be clear on this. I've been invited to stay. I can't refuse.

EILEEN. Oh yes, you can.

BOB (*sitting on settee*). Well, I'm not going to.

EILEEN. You're not?

BOB. No.

EILEEN. Bob, don't you realize Dad wants to make all he can out of you?

BOB. But I shall make something out of it, too. The more I become an expert in model-making, the more Lightcraft lathes—even complete workshops—I'll be selling.

EILEEN. But he's not thinking of you.

BOB. He's not?

EILEEN. He's only out to exploit you. Understand? Exploit you.

BOB (*reacting exactly like* FRED). Exploit me?

EILEEN. Yes.

BOB (*rising. Talking exactly like* FRED *and making some of his gestures*). Now let's view this in perspective, shall we, Eileen? Let's see it all fair and square.

EILEEN (*horrified*). What?

> (FRED *enters from the wings and stands in the french windows. He listens to the following approvingly. At some point in the speech* FRED *and* BOB *fold their arms simultaneously and identically.*)

BOB. As I see it, it's a basic characteristic of living things to exploit each other. We've got a most complex biological sanction, for it— so it's not for the likes of us to go against nature—now is it?

EILEEN (*moving* D.L. *Horrified. To audience*). He's beginning to talk like him!

BOB. Who is?

EILEEN. You are!

BOB (*pleased*). Like your father?

EILEEN. In a few years, I won't be able to tell one from the other.

BOB. But that's splendid!

EILEEN (*horrified*). Splendid?

BOB. Why, what's wrong?

EILEEN (*moving to* BOB). What's wrong? I hate the sight of him, that's all.

BOB (*amazed*). Hate your father?

EILEEN. Yes!

> (FRED *moves rapidly in between* EILEEN *and* BOB.)

FRED (*clapping his hands*). Beautiful, Eileen! Beautiful! First class! (*To audience.*) It's nice to know she's getting it out of her system at last.

EILEEN (*aghast*). It's you?

FRED. Yes, it's me—your dear old reactionary dad.

EILEEN. You heard?

FRED (*smiles*). I heard.

EILEEN. I'm not sorry.

FRED (*smiles*). 'course not.

EILEEN. Exploiter!

FRED (*nods and smiles*). Well—yes.

EILEEN. Juggler!

FRED (*nods and smiles*). Sometimes.

EILEEN. Cheat!

FRED (*nods and smiles*). Occasionally.

EILEEN. Liar!

FRED. Tut-tut-tut! You beautiful little rebel, you! Now what's all the trouble about?

EILEEN. I'm not having Bob live under this roof.

FRED. But he's been invited.

EILEEN. I don't care. (*Emphatically.*) We are not going to live here.

FRED. I see.

EILEEN. If he loves me, he'll come with me.

FRED. Where?

EILEEN. You know where—the Dragon Hotel—until we find a flat together.

FRED (*tragically*). That's that, then. I shan't argue. If you feel that way, I must not interfere. (*Turning to* BOB.) Well, Bob, my son—

BOB. Yes?

FRED. She's asking you to desert your newly-found family—but if you love her, you'd better go.

BOB (*gulps*). I know.

FRED. Disgrace and humiliation lie ahead of you. Living in sin—in public! Divorce—no job—no prospects—no friends—but if you love her, you'd better do it.

BOB (*gulps*). I know.

FRED (*putting his hand on* BOB's *shoulder as a farewell gesture and then moving slighty* U.S.). Of course, I should miss you—I had great hopes for the pair of us. What a future we might have had— What a future! But if you truly love her—

EILEEN (*to* BOB). Well?

BOB (*weakly to* EILEEN). Are you sure we'd get on together?

EILEEN (*furious*). Get on together? After all last week! (*Spits out.*) Get back to your locos!

BOB. But, Eileen, I—

FRED (*bounding in between the pair of them and attacking* BOB). You traitor! You dog! Scoundrel! Viper! Cur!
(BOB *backs towards the french windows.*)
BOB. But, Mr. Midway—
FRED (*forcing him to the french window imperiously*). You heard what my daughter said! Get back to the locos! (*Sotto. Urgent.*) Mr. Makepiece is down there. He's asking about the lathe. Get in, lad. Here's your opportunity! (*Imperiously.*) Get back to the locos! At once! I'll have no arguments!
BOB. Right! (*He moves off.*)
FRED (*shouts after him*). It's all you're good for! (*Moving to* EILEEN D.R., *he sighs, relieved, and mops his brow.*) Thank goodness, Eileen. You found him out in the nick of time— He'd be no good to you, you know. He's simply on the make. Not a scrap of real tender love in him— (*Turning on the "deep", "sincere" emotional stuff.*) Eileen! If you've never taken your father's advice before—take it now.
EILEEN. What?
FRED. Find yourself a man that really suits you: a poverty-stricken bohemian—a hippy, a failure, a victim of society—someone you can care for.
EILEEN. You mean that?
FRED (*with a mockery that the audience recognizes, but* EILEEN *doesn't*). I'm emptying my heart. A down and out—a derelict—someone who is utterly truthful, utterly honest, utterly loving— In other words, a man who has no hope of success in this world. In the final analysis, that is your type. Collect your case! Go to the Dragon Hotel—or the back streets of Bayswater—wherever it may be—and find him.
EILEEN. You want me to do that?
FRED. Look at me, my child. I know you. However painful it is for me to admit it—you need a man whose worthiness can match yours. It's your future happiness we must think of now.
EILEEN. Father, I've never heard you talk like this before.
FRED (*ushering her to the hall door. Mock tragic*). I know when I'm defeated. Take my advice. No matter how sordid your life, remember one thing: if it makes you happy, it will make me joyous. (*He closes the door on her. Now alone, he shows plainly that it is a trick. Moving up* L.) Phew! Will it work? Will it work, I wonder?
(HILDA *enters, carrying* TOM'S *trousers and a sewing-basket.* FRED *sees the door opening and cries:*)
Believe me, Eileen— (*Aware of his mistake.*) Oh, it's you.
HILDA. I passed Eileen on the stairs. She says she's off.

FRED. Yes.

HILDA (*alarmed*). She's not going to live here with Bob?

FRED. No.

HILDA. She's not?

FRED. I said "No", but don't worry.

HILDA (*upset*). You mean we'll have to disown her, after all?

FRED. Maybe yes—maybe no. We'll see.

HILDA (*sits in chair* R. *and starts sewing*). Well, I only hope you know what you're doing.

(TOM *enters.*)

TOM. Have you spoken to Mr. Makepiece?

FRED (*sitting on settee*). I have, Tom—and it's all been settled.

TOM (*at* R. *of settee*). In my absence?

FRED. In your absence.

TOM. Well, what have you decided, Fred?

FRED. We've decided that you and your future bride are going to emigrate.

TOM. Emigrate? Me?

FRED. And her.

TOM. But I don't want to.

FRED. You will—when you receive the money.

TOM. What money?

FRED. Mr. Makepiece is making you a special grant for permament residence abroad. Most generous and lavish, I'd say.

TOM. Oh well, if it's substantial—

FRED. Now you know I wouldn't fail you as far as money's concerned—especially if it's someone else's.

TOM. Well, thanks, Fred—

FRED. Don't mention it, Tom.

TOM. I'd better go and break the news to Daphne.

FRED. Yes, Tom. Invite her round here tonight.

TOM (*moving to the hall door*). Right, Fred. (*He leaves.*)

FRED (*reflects*). We'll discuss how quickly we can export the pair of you.

(*During the following* TOM *wheels his motor-bike off stage.*)

HILDA (*slightly tearful*). I'm not so sure I want him to be exported.

FRED. It's sad to lose him, but we must view it realistically.

(MAKEPIECE *enters through the french windows.*)

(*Rising.*) There you are, Mr. Makepiece. (*The motor-bike starts up off stage.*) You hear that sound? It's my son—off to reclaim the young lady in question. My wife joins me in thanking you for the noble sacrifice you have made.

MAKEPIECE (*curtly*). Don't mention it. Well, I must be going. (*Crossing to* HILDA.) Good day.

HILDA (*rising and shaking hands*). Good day, Mr. Makepiece.
    (*During the following* MRS. HADFIELD *walks up the drive.*)

MAKEPIECE (*offering his hand*). Good day, Midway.

FRED (*shaking hands. Urgently*). There are some important things we haven't discussed.

MAKEPIECE (*moving to hall door*). Such as?

FRED (*following him desperately*). Have you anyone in mind for insuring the town redevelopment, for example?

MAKEPIECE (*about to leave*). Another time, perhaps.
                    (*The chimes ring.*)

HILDA (*moving to the window*). It's Mrs. Hadfield.

MAKEPIECE (*horrified*). Mrs. Hadfield? Did you say Mrs. Hadfield? My sister?

HILDA. Yes, I'll let her in.

MAKEPIECE (*moving down to* R. *of settee*). Wait a minute. I'd prefer not to see her. She's bound to ask me why I'm here—and it could be rather embarrassing.

FRED (*moving to* U.L. *Beams*). Then why not step back into our little garden?

MAKEPIECE (*moving to french windows and turning with a sudden thought*). Oh dear. That car of mine out there will give the game away— she's bound to know I'm here. What will you tell her?

FRED (*clapping his hand to his forehead with feigned perplexity*). What will we tell her, Mother? What will we tell her? (*To* MAKEPIECE *brightly*.) Let's say you've come round here on behalf of the Council to consult me on insuring the total town redevelopment. How's that?
            (*Pause.* MAKEPIECE *hesitates. The chimes ring again.*)

MAKEPIECE (*swallows*). You'd better! (*He bolts into the garden.*)

FRED. Saved by the ding-dong! Go on, Mother, let her in. (*He glances upwards and says slowly and modestly.*) The total town re-development? Insured by the Sunlight? That's more than even I could have hoped for!
            (MRS. HADFIELD *enters and moves to* R. *of settee. She is followed by* HILDA, *who moves to front window.*)

MRS. HADFIELD. Is that my brother's car outside? Is he here?

FRED. Yes—he happens to be down the garden, studying the locos. I asked him to come over to settle that trifling difference between his nephew and my daughter—and I must say he's done it extremely well.

MRS. HADFIELD. You mean that Avril will be returning to Nigel?

FRED. With his uncle's blessing plus his readmission to the family fortune.

MRS. HADFIELD (*overjoyed*). You mean he's put him back in the will?

FRED. Exactly.

MRS. HADFIELD (*sharply*). Well, I thought you'd have to scheme something like that before you let her return.

FRED (*jovially*). You're not worried about it, Mrs. Hadfield—neither are our children. (*He opens the kitchen door.*) Come out, you naughty pair—you naughty, naughty pair!

> (NIGEL *and* AVRIL *come out.* AVRIL *is fastening the top button of her dress.* NIGEL's *hair is out of place and his collar and tie are awry.* FRED *moves* D.L.)

MRS. HADFIELD (*moving to* NIGEL). Nigel, what have you done? Nigel! (*She adjusts his collar and tie.*)

> (AVRIL *moves to her father.*)

AVRIL (*confidentially*). Well, there has to be a bit of give and take, doesn't there—and now I know his uncle's going on with the giving—

FRED. Quite right, Avril—quite right!

AVRIL (*moving across* R. *to* HILDA). We'll be going, then. Me and Niggy can cuddle a bit more comfy in our little nest. (*Over her shoulder to* NIGEL.) Can't we, Niggy? (*To* HILDA.) I shall never forgive him for his carryings-on, Mom— (*Moving to him.*) but I must say it's brought out his roguish side a bit.

MRS. HADFIELD. Nigel! Shall we go? (*She moves into the hall.*)

AVRIL. Cheerio, Mom. Cheerio, Dad.

HILDA. See you both next month.

AVRIL. That's right— After church.

> (AVRIL *moves into the hall.*)

NIGEL. Good-bye, Mother. Good-bye, Father.

> (AVRIL *returns, grabs* NIGEL's *arm and pulls him out of the room.*)

AVRIL (*to* NIGEL). Come along, you filthy beast!

> (AVRIL, NIGEL *and* MRS. HADFIELD *leave by the front door.* HILDA *looks through the window and waves to* AVRIL.)

HILDA. Good-bye! Good-bye! (*She turns and says rapturously to* FRED.) They're together again.

FRED (*moving to* L.C.). Yes—and by this time Tom will be with his Daphne. That's another pair we've put on the straight and narrow.

HILDA (*moving to* R.C.). That only leaves Bob and Eileen.

FRED. Bob will be staying here. He'll be like another son.

HILDA (*anxiously*). But Eileen? What will happen to Eileen? If she goes to that Dragon Hotel, we'll have to disclaim her!

FRED (*mock pathetic*). Perhaps— Go and fetch her, Mother— Tell her I want to say "Good-bye". It's the only way.

(HILDA *nods tearfully and leaves.* FRED *moves to the french window, but* MAKEPIECE *is already entering.*)

MAKEPIECE. They've gone?

FRED (*urgently*). Now, Mr. Makepiece, there's something I want to talk over with you.

MAKEPIECE (*brusquely*). I'm afraid I haven't the time.

FRED. As an insurance man—

MAKEPIECE (*moving briskly round the front of the settee and towards the hall door*). If it's insurance, come to my office tomorrow—

FRED (*following after him*). I've sold a good many life policies in my time—

MAKEPIECE. I'm sure you have, but I must say "good day".

FRED. —and I've got a proposition which could be of interest to you.

MAKEPIECE. Believe me, there are no propositions left—I've considered them—bought them—or rejected them.

FRED. But, Mr. Makepiece—

MAKEPIECE. No "buts"—I've so little time. I must go. Good day. (*He opens the door into the hall and is about to leave.*)

FRED. I know how to lengthen your life expectation.

(*Pause.* MAKEPIECE *freezes with his back to the audience. He turns.* FRED *with a confident smile has moved to* c.)

MAKEPIECE. You what? Lengthen my life? (*Urgently. Almost trembling, moving to* FRED.) Then tell me. If there's something, tell me! Is it new on the market? If it isn't new on the market, I've already had it.

FRED (*whispers*). Close the door.

MAKEPIECE. Yes, certainly. (*He does so obediently.*) Now what is it? (*Rapidly and frightened.*) Is it Monkey Gland? I've had Monkey Gland. I've also had Rabbit's Blood, Lions' Sperm and Queen Bee Jelly. Last year I went for three doses of Rams' Injections in Switzerland. It increased the vigour somewhat—I'm sure it increased the vigour— At least, I think so.

(FRED *beckons to him with his head to follow him to the extreme* D.L. *corner of the stage.* MAKEPIECE *does so.*)

(*Whispers urgently.*) Well?

FRED (*whispers darkly and secretly*). I'm an insurance man.

MAKEPIECE. Yes?

FRED. In my trade, you have to know how to sum them up.

MAKEPIECE. Of course—yes, you must.

FRED. No good letting them have a policy—one premium and then—
phut.

MAKEPIECE. What have you discovered?

FRED. It varies from man to man.

MAKEPIECE. Oh?

FRED. With you—

MAKEPIECE. Yes?

FRED. Be careful with the women.

MAKEPIECE. You mean—never again?

FRED. Not with people like that Daphne. Too young. Too (*Shrugs.*)—
you know.

MAKEPIECE. Yes—yes, she was.

FRED. Mind and body must go together. Overdo one of them and—
(*He snaps his fingers.*)

MAKEPIECE. Well?

FRED. You want a woman between—twenty-five and thirty, say.

MAKEPIECE. Uh-huh.

FRED. Someone who's perhaps rather soulful and sincere.

MAKEPIECE. Yes—yes?

FRED. Someone who'll gladly suffer for the cause of truth—as long as
she knows where the next meal's coming from.

MAKEPIECE (*excited*). I'm with you.

FRED. Someone who'll give you a constant mental challenge—
Keep you brisk— Keep you alive!

MAKEPIECE (*smiling*). Marvellous!

FRED. Above all, a woman who'll never be an embarrassment—an
encumbrance. And as she won't try to hang on to you—you might
find yourself hanging on to her.

MAKEPIECE. Yes, but where could I find a woman like that?
(*The door opens and* EILEEN *enters, followed by* HILDA. EILEEN
moves to R.C. *and puts down her suitcase.* HILDA *stays* U.R.)

FRED (*to* MAKEPIECE). You haven't met my daughter, have you?

EILEEN. Father— Good-bye!

HILDA. You mustn't let her go, Fred—you mustn't!
(FRED *says the following emotionally and rhetorically to obtain a
satisfactory but different response from each one of his listeners.*)

FRED. Hilda! Me and our Eileen have had a heart-to-heart. You must
learn to recognize, as I have, Mother—her world is not ours. We
are lost in the abyss of expediency and compromise—but our Eileen
has a pure, inner radiance which we cannot deny—and to which we
must all of us capitulate.

EILEEN. I'm sorry, Mother. I've made up my mind. I'm not going to live a life of lies!

FRED (*aside to* MAKEPIECE). Soulful and sincere! Mark that!

HILDA (*moving to* D.R.). Eileen! Do be careful what you say in front of Mr. Makepiece. He might take you seriously.

FRED. Don't you understand, Mother—Eileen is beyond our subterfuge. Does it matter who hears her? She is free. She has nothing to hide from anybody. Isn't that so, Eileen?

EILEEN (*unsure*). Well—er—yes.

FRED. Speak out your mind then, my daughter. Every word you say is a joyful penance for me.

EILEEN (*moving slightly to* HILDA). Mother, I'm going to stay at the Dragon Hotel until I find a flat somewhere. Try to understand, Mother. I loved Bob fully, utterly—but obviously he didn't love me, not in that way. And once a woman starts doubting whether she can ever find a pure and unselfish love, then—

HILDA. Then what?

FRED. Courage, Eileen! Don't disappoint me! Speak on!

EILEEN. —then it doesn't really matter who she gives her body to.

HILDA (*aghast*). Eileen!

FRED (*aside to* MAKEPIECE). That's what you might call suffering in the cause of truth!

EILEEN. Disown me, Mother, if you wish. In any case, I'm not needed here. And my pride will never allow me to be an encumbrance to anyone!

FRED (*aside to* MAKEPIECE). "An encumbrance!" What did I tell you? (*To* EILEEN.) Splendid, Eileen! Splendid! (*He claps his hands.*)

EILEEN. Good-bye. (*She picks up her case and moves to hall door.*)

MAKEPIECE. Just one moment— (*Moving to* EILEEN.) Would you allow me to give you a lift?

HILDA (*hurriedly*). Mr. Makepiece! You're such a busy man!

MAKEPIECE (*to* HILDA). I think I've got the time to spare. (*To* EILEEN.) Well?

EILEEN. Why not? (*She gives him the suitcase and moves into the hall.*)

MAKEPIECE (*amazed at his good fortune*). A most fascinating family! Good day! (*He moves jauntily into the hall to join* EILEEN.)

HILDA (*panic-stricken*). Fred! What shall we do? What shall we do?

FRED (*moving to* C.). Don't worry, Mother— Look through the window.

(MAKEPIECE *and* EILEEN *are now walking out of the door and down the path into the wings.* HILDA *moves to the window.*)

HILDA (*amazed*). Father! He's taken her arm! What will the neighbours think if they see?

FRED. Not to worry, Mother. The friends of Caesar are above suspicion. (*Sits on settee.*) Look again!

HILDA (*amazed*). Our Eileen doesn't seem to mind. (*Turns to* FRED.) She's smiling at him!

FRED (*mock disappointment*). And I told her to go and get herself a penniless, pure-hearted beatnik! (*With almost simple, childish pleasure at his cunning.*) I knew she'd do the opposite—if only to spite her dad. (*With admiration.*) Oh, she's a beautiful little rebel, that one!

HILDA (*moving to* FRED *at* D.C.). What do you make of it, Fred?

(FRED *and* HILDA *say the following wistfully and sentimentally staring out at the audience.*)

FRED. What? Him the Establishment—and her the Honest Intellectual? (*Sadly.*) Tut-tut-tut. They don't belong round here, Mother.

HILDA. They don't?

FRED. There's so few in these parts, they're bound to get together if only to keep each other warm.

HILDA. You think they'll be finding their own little nest, then?

(FRED *nods slowly. Then during* HILDA's *next speech he lowers his head.*)

Fancy! (*Pause.*) It's a wonderful world, Fred.

FRED (*raises his head and while doing so says in a neutral tone to the audience*). Is it?

HILDA. And you're such a wonderful man.

FRED (*in a colourless voice*). I'd better do the lawn.

HILDA. Yes. Yes, you'd better—'cos we don't want any talk, do we?

(FRED *and* HILDA *nod to each other, then turn and move rapidly to the two doors.* HILDA *goes out through the kitchen door,* FRED *through the hall door. The doors close simultaneously.*)

CURTAIN

PROPERTY PLOT

ACT ONE

At curtain rise
  Duster used by Hilda. Thereafter
    placed in apron pocket for future
    use
In Fred's pocket
  Pipe and matches
On table c. behind settee
  Crumb tray and brush
  Cigarette box with one cigarette,
    lighter, box of chocolates
*Fixed on back wall between the two
doors*
  Inter-com telephone set
Chair L.
  Cushion
Window table R.
  Ash tray with stub and ash
Bookshelves L.
  Set of *Encyclopedia Britannica*
  Large book files

  Small seven-inch record in sleeve
Television table R.
  Large blueprints
Chest of drawers U.L.
  Small tray
Offstage R.
  Lawn mower and oil can (FRED)
  Several Sunday newspapers (TOM)
  Suitcase (FILEEN)
  Handbag (AVRIL)
  Handbag (MRS. HADFIELD)
In garage
  Tin of car polish and duster (TOM)
  Motor-bike (TOM)
Kitchen
  Vase of flowers (HILDA)
  Tray containing tea and biscuits for
    four (HILDA)
Hall
  Pair of trousers (TOM)

ACT TWO

Chair R.
  Pouffe to left of it

Fixed on back wall between the two doors
  Inter-com telephone set

Chest of drawers U.L.
  Prayer Book inside drawer

Cabinet U.R.
  Vase
Offstage: hall
  Pair of trousers (TOM)
  Bundle of zip fasteners (TOM)
Right
  Passenger trolley railway (FRED)

ACT THREE

In FRED's pocket
  Cigar
In TOM's pocket
  Matches
Bookshelves L.
  Gramophone records, small clock
Back wall U.L.
  Picture
On television table R.
  Ash tray, ceramic figure of cat

c. on table behind settee
  Sunday newspaper
Extreme R.
  Motor-bike (TOM)
Offstage: hall
  TOM's trousers and workbox con-
    taining zip fasteners, needle,
    cotton, thimble and scissors
    (HILDA)
  Suitcase (EILEEN)
  Handbag (MRS. HADFIELD)